Grade 2

Scott Foresman

# Grammar and Writing
# Practice Book

PEARSON
Scott Foresman

**Editorial Offices:** Glenview, Illinois • Parsippany, New Jersey • New York, New York
**Sales Offices:** Boston, Massachusetts • Duluth, Georgia • Glenview, Illinois
Coppell, Texas • Sacramento, California • Mesa, Arizona

-4

**Education, Inc.**

inted in the United States of America. This publication,
used with appropriate equipment to reproduce copies

1 10 09 08 07

# Unit 1  Exploration

# Unit 2  Working Together

# Unit 3  Creative Ideas

# Unit 4  Our Changing World

# Unit 5  Responsibility

# Unit 6  Traditions

## Grammar Extra Practice

## Standardized Test Preparation

## Unit Writing Lessons

# Grammar Lessons

Name _____

# Sentences

A **sentence** is a group of words that tells a complete idea. The words are in an order that makes sense. A sentence begins with a capital letter. Many sentences end with a **period (.)**.

I have many friends.  ← This is a complete sentence.

many friends  ← This is not a complete sentence.

---

**Find** the sentence. **Write** the sentence.

1. a friend                    I have a friend.

_____

- - - - - - - - - - - - - - - - - - - - - - - - - -

_____

2. We climbed a tree.          climbed a tree

_____

- - - - - - - - - - - - - - - - - - - - - - - - - -

_____

3. Walter is my friend.        is my friend

_____

- - - - - - - - - - - - - - - - - - - - - - - - - -

_____

4. my grandpa                  I love my grandpa.

_____

- - - - - - - - - - - - - - - - - - - - - - - - - -

_____

5. Walter has a pony.          has a pony

_____

- - - - - - - - - - - - - - - - - - - - - - - - - -

_____

© Pearson Education

**School-Home CONNECTION**

**Home Activity** Your child learned about sentences. Read a story together. Have your child point out a sentence and tell what capital letter it begins with and what punctuation mark is at the end.

# Sentences

**Write** the name of your friend.

_____
- - - - - - - - - - - - - - - - - - - - - - - - - -
_____

**Write** sentences about what you and your friend do.

_____
- - - - - - - - - - - - - - - - - - - - - - - - - -
_____
- - - - - - - - - - - - - - - - - - - - - - - - - -
_____
- - - - - - - - - - - - - - - - - - - - - - - - - -
_____
- - - - - - - - - - - - - - - - - - - - - - - - - -
_____

**Draw** a picture of you and your friend doing something together.

**School-Home CONNECTION**   **Home Activity** Your child learned how to use sentences in writing. Have your child write two sentences about what he or she likes to do with a friend. Make sure each sentence begins with a capital letter and ends with a period.

© Pearson Education

# Sentences

**Mark** the words that complete each sentence.

1. The children ____
   - ○ **A** rode a pony.
   - ○ **B** corn.
   - ○ **C** ice cream.

2. Iris and Walter ____
   - ○ **A** grass.
   - ○ **B** beautiful day.
   - ○ **C** are friends.

3. I ____
   - ○ **A** cold day.
   - ○ **B** play with friends.
   - ○ **C** blue chair.

4. Grandpa ____
   - ○ **A** snowy winter.
   - ○ **B** lives in the country.
   - ○ **C** telephone.

5. The city ____
   - ○ **A** has many people.
   - ○ **B** fire.
   - ○ **C** day off.

6. The boy ____
   - ○ **A** lettuce patch.
   - ○ **B** movie star.
   - ○ **C** makes a tree house.

**Home Activity** Your child prepared for taking tests on sentences. Have your child tell you three sentences about his or her day.

**Grammar and Writing Practice Book**　　　　　Unit 1　Week 1　**Day 4**　**3**

# Sentences

**Find** the sentence. **Circle** the sentence.

1. I have five friends.     five friends

2. played ball     My friends played ball.

3. the game     We like the game.

**Write** each sentence on the line.
**Begin** and **end** the sentence correctly.

4. we took a pony ride

_____
- - - - - - - - - - - - - - - - - - - -
_____

5. the city is noisy

_____
- - - - - - - - - - - - - - - - - - - -
_____

6. i want a tree house

_____
- - - - - - - - - - - - - - - - - - - -
_____

**School-Home CONNECTION**

**Home Activity** Your child reviewed sentences. Offer a sentence starter, such as *Our home, Your mother,* or *A big tree,* and have your child use it in a complete sentence.

© Pearson Education

# Subjects

The **subject** of a sentence tells who or what does something.

> The **astronaut** went to the moon.
>
> **Mike** talks to the astronaut.

**Write** the subject of each sentence.

1. The astronauts used a telescope.

   _____

   - - - - - - - - - - - - - - - - - -

   _____

2. Spaceships circle the Earth.

   _____

   - - - - - - - - - - - - - - - - - -

   _____

3. Men flew in a spaceship.

   _____

   - - - - - - - - - - - - - - - - - -

   _____

4. The moon shines at night.

   _____

   - - - - - - - - - - - - - - - - - -

   _____

5. A space shuttle lands like an airplane.

   _____

   - - - - - - - - - - - - - - - - - -

© Pearson Education

**School-Home CONNECTION**

**Home Activity** Your child learned about the subjects of sentences. Read a story together. Point to simple sentences in the story. Ask your child to tell you the subject of each sentence.

# Subjects

**Write** four sentences about the planets or space travel.
**Use** words from the box or words of your own.
**Circle** the subject in each sentence.

| | | | |
|---|---|---|---|
| Jupiter | sun | rocket ship | astronauts |
| Mars | moon | shuttle | Earth |

_____

- - - - - - - - - - - - - - - - - -

_____

- - - - - - - - - - - - - - - - - -

_____

- - - - - - - - - - - - - - - - - -

_____

- - - - - - - - - - - - - - - - - -

© Pearson Education

**Home Activity** Your child learned how to use the subjects of sentences in writing. Have your child write two sentences about astronauts and underline the subjects of the sentences.

# Subjects

Mark the letter of the subject that completes each sentence.

1. ____ is an astronaut.
   ○ **A** Seeing
   ○ **B** Paula
   ○ **C** Fun

2. ____ have hard jobs.
   ○ **A** Astronauts
   ○ **B** And
   ○ **C** Watch

3. ____ is a big star.
   ○ **A** Chair
   ○ **B** Leaves
   ○ **C** The sun

4. ____ is a planet.
   ○ **A** Jack
   ○ **B** Mars
   ○ **C** Play

5. ____ is our home.
   ○ **A** The chair
   ○ **B** Tell
   ○ **C** The Earth

6. ____ sees the stars.
   ○ **A** Maya
   ○ **B** Sit
   ○ **C** Have

**Home Activity** Your child prepared for taking tests on the subjects of sentences. Say simple sentences such as *The moon is full. The sun is hot. The Earth is round.* Then ask your child to tell you the subjects of the sentences.

# Subjects

**Underline** the subject in each sentence.

1. The planets are far away.

2. The sun is a ball of gas.

3. Astronauts wear spacesuits.

**Write** a subject to complete each sentence.
**Use** a subject from the box.

| The moon | An astronaut | Spaceships |
|---|---|---|

4. _____ are faster than airplanes.

5. _____ looks like a face.

6. _____ walks on the moon.

**Home Activity** Your child reviewed the subjects of sentences. Give your child a phrase such as *A cat* or *The door* and have your child use it as the subject of a sentence.

© Pearson Education

# Predicates

The **predicate** tells what the subject of a sentence does or is.

We **drive to the woods.**
The family **hikes.**

_____

**Write** the predicate of each sentence.

1. My family makes a camp.

_____
- - - - - - - - - - - - - - - - - - - - -
_____

2. Dad and I set up the tent.

_____
- - - - - - - - - - - - - - - - - - - - -
_____

3. The tent falls down.

_____
- - - - - - - - - - - - - - - - - - - - -
_____

4. The rain pours.

_____
- - - - - - - - - - - - - - - - - - - - -
_____

5. We sleep in the car.

_____
- - - - - - - - - - - - - - - - - - - - -
_____

© Pearson Education

**Home Activity** Your child learned about the predicates of sentences. Read a story together. Point out simple sentences in the story. Ask your child to tell you the predicate of each sentence.

# Predicates

**Tell** about a time when you went on a hike or a walk.
**Circle** the predicates in your sentences.

_____

- - - - - - - - - - - - - - - - - - - - - - - - -

_____

- - - - - - - - - - - - - - - - - - - - - - - - -

_____

_____

- - - - - - - - - - - - - - - - - - - - - - - - -

_____

_____

- - - - - - - - - - - - - - - - - - - - - - - - -

_____

_____

- - - - - - - - - - - - - - - - - - - - - - - - -

_____

© Pearson Education

**School-Home CONNECTION**  **Home Activity** Your child learned how to use the predicates of sentences in writing. Have your child write you a note and ask him or her to circle the predicate in each sentence.

# Predicates

**Mark** the letter of the predicate that completes each sentence.

1. We ____
   ○ **A** hiked.
   ○ **B** in the woods.
   ○ **C** Mom and I.

2. My dad and I ____
   ○ **A** good food.
   ○ **B** saw a snake.
   ○ **C** my sister.

3. A campfire ____
   ○ **A** his friend.
   ○ **B** is fun.
   ○ **C** and loud.

4. The stew ____
   ○ **A** tastes good.
   ○ **B** cold rain.
   ○ **C** tired.

5. The lake ____
   ○ **A** cats and dogs.
   ○ **B** that time.
   ○ **C** has many fish.

6. Dad ____
   ○ **A** on the trail.
   ○ **B** catches a fish.
   ○ **C** a hot pan.

**School-Home CONNECTION**

**Home Activity** Your child prepared for taking tests on predicates of sentences. Have your child write several sentences about something your family did together. Ask your child to underline the predicate in each sentence.

# Predicates

**Write** the predicate of each sentence.

1. My family looks for butterflies.

_____
- - - - - - - - - - - - - - - - - - - - - - - -
_____

2. I see big yellow ones.

_____
- - - - - - - - - - - - - - - - - - - - - - - -
_____

3. Mom points to little red ones.

_____
- - - - - - - - - - - - - - - - - - - - - - - -
_____

**Write** a predicate to complete each sentence.
**Use** a predicate from the box.

| is in second grade | look for rocks |

_____
- - - - - - - - - - - - - - - - - - - - - - - -
4. Rosa and her dad _____.

_____
- - - - - - - - - - - - - - - - - - - - - - - -
5. Rosa _____.

**Home Activity** Your child reviewed the predicates of sentences. Read a newspaper article together. Find simple sentences in the article. Have your child underline the predicates of the sentences.

© Pearson Education

# Statements and Questions

A **statement** is a sentence that tells something. A statement ends with a **period (.)**.

A desert is a very dry place**.**

A **question** is a sentence that asks something. A question ends with a **question mark (?)**.

What grows in a desert**?**

All statements and questions begin with capital letters.

---

**Put** a period at the end if the sentence is a statement.
**Put** a question mark at the end if the sentence is a question.

1. Have you seen a desert_____

2. A desert is beautiful_____

3. What lives in the desert_____

4. Plants grow in the desert_____

5. Do animals live in the desert_____

6. Tortoises live there_____

**Home Activity** Your child learned about statements and questions. Choose one of your child's favorite books. Point to a sentence and ask your child whether the sentence is a statement or a question. Ask your child to tell you why.

# Statements and Questions

**Write** two statements and two questions about this picture.

_____

- - - - - - - - - - - - - - - - - - - - - - - - - - -

_____

_____

- - - - - - - - - - - - - - - - - - - - - - - - - - -

_____

_____

- - - - - - - - - - - - - - - - - - - - - - - - - - -

_____

_____

- - - - - - - - - - - - - - - - - - - - - - - - - - -

_____

© Pearson Education

**School-Home CONNECTION**

**Home Activity** Your child learned how to use statements and questions in writing. Tell your child to imagine that you are going on a trip to the desert. Ask your child to write a statement and a question about the trip.

# Statements and Questions

**Mark** the correct sentence in each group.

1. ○ **A** lizards like the heat?
   ○ **B** lizards like the heat.
   ○ **C** Lizards like the heat.

2. ○ **A** most cactuses grow flowers.
   ○ **B** Most cactuses grow flowers.
   ○ **C** most cactuses grow flowers?

3. ○ **A** Do zebras live in the desert?
   ○ **B** do zebras live in the desert?
   ○ **C** Do zebras live in the desert.

4. ○ **A** a jack rabbit has long legs?
   ○ **B** a jack rabbit has long legs.
   ○ **C** A jack rabbit has long legs.

5. ○ **A** does it rain in the desert.
   ○ **B** Does it rain in the desert?
   ○ **C** Does it rain in the desert.

6. ○ **A** Can a desert be cold.
   ○ **B** can a desert be cold?
   ○ **C** Can a desert be cold?

**Home Activity** Your child prepared for taking tests on statements and questions. As you watch television with your child, have him or her point out statements and questions that occur in dialogue.

© Pearson Education

# Statements and Questions

**Write** each sentence correctly.

**1.** i talked to a gardener named Billy

_____

- - - - - - - - - - - - - - - - - - - - - - - -

_____

**2.** will you plant me a lily

_____

- - - - - - - - - - - - - - - - - - - - - - - -

_____

**3.** can you grow it tonight

_____

- - - - - - - - - - - - - - - - - - - - - - - -

_____

**4.** i must catch a flight

_____

- - - - - - - - - - - - - - - - - - - - - - - -

_____

**5.** the desert can often be chilly

_____

- - - - - - - - - - - - - - - - - - - - - - - -

_____

**Home Activity** Your child reviewed statements and questions. Choose a story to read to your child. Say a sentence that is a statement or a question and have your child tell which it is. Continue with other sentences.

© Pearson Education

# Commands and Exclamations

A **command** is a sentence that tells someone to do something.
It ends with a **period (.)**.
The subject of a command is *you*, but *you* is usually not shown.

    Find the strongest one.        Please answer me.

An **exclamation** is a sentence that shows surprise or shows strong feelings. It ends with an **exclamation mark (!)**.

    Ouch! I tripped on that rock!   What a great idea this is!

All commands and exclamations begin with capital letters.

---

**Write *C*** if the sentence is a command.
**Write *E*** if it is an exclamation.

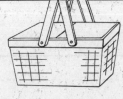

1. Get me a basket. _____

2. That is a huge basket! _____

3. Put in the food. _____

4. Bring the ants. _____

5. Oh, no, I dropped the food! _____

**Home Activity** Your child learned about commands and exclamations. Play the following game with your child: Set a time limit of two minutes and during that time talk to each other strusing only commands and exclamations.

Name _____

# Commands and Exclamations

**Imagine** that you are a character in the story.
**Tell** why you are the strongest one.
**Use** a command and an exclamation.

_____

- - - - - - - - - - - - - - - - -

_____

_____

- - - - - - - - - - - - - - - - -

_____

_____

- - - - - - - - - - - - - - - - -

_____

_____

- - - - - - - - - - - - - - - - -

_____

_____

- - - - - - - - - - - - - - - - -

_____

**Home Activity** Your child learned about how to use commands and exclamations in writing sentences. Have your child write commands and exclamations on sticky notes and post them in appropriate places, for example, a note on the refrigerator that says *I am hungry!*

© Pearson Education

# Commands and Exclamations

**Mark** the correct sentence in each group.

1. ○ **A** You are very strong!
   ○ **B** you are very strong.
   ○ **C** You are very strong

2. ○ **A** blow out the match.
   ○ **B** Blow out the match.
   ○ **C** blow out the match!

3. ○ **A** shoot the arrow!
   ○ **B** shoot the arrow.
   ○ **C** Shoot the arrow.

4. ○ **A** catch the cat!
   ○ **B** Catch the cat.
   ○ **C** catch the cat.

5. ○ **A** The wind chased me!
   ○ **B** the wind chased me!
   ○ **C** the wind chased me.

6. ○ **A** the rock is the strongest!
   ○ **B** the rock is the strongest.
   ○ **C** The rock is the strongest!

**Home Activity** Your child prepared for taking tests on commands and exclamations. With your child, look through a magazine and find and mark five examples each of commands snd exclamations.

© Pearson Education

# Commands and Exclamations

Write *C* if the sentence is a command.
Write *E* if it is an exclamation.

1. Knock on the door. _____

2. Come in the house. _____

3. Wow! I'm afraid of the dark! _____

**Write** each sentence correctly.

4. push the rock

_____

_____

5. look at Ant

_____

_____

6. how strong Ant is

_____

_____

**Home Activity** Your child reviewed commands and exclamations. Write the commands and exclamations from this page on index cards. Hold up a card. Have your child read the sentence and tell whether it is a command or an exclamation.

# Nouns

A **noun** names a person, place, animal, or thing.

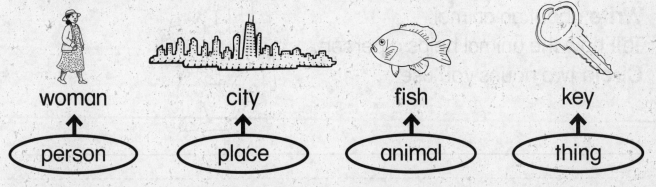

| woman | city | fish | key |
|---|---|---|---|
| person | place | animal | thing |

**Write** the noun in each sentence.

1. The man fell down. _____

2. The ice cracked. _____

3. The dog barked. _____

**Write** the two nouns in each sentence.

4. The cat is in a tree.

_____  _____

5. The boy gets a ladder.

_____  _____

 **Home Activity** Your child learned about nouns. Take a walk with your child. Point to people, places, animals, and things without naming them. Have your child tell you each noun.

© Pearson Education

# Nouns

How can animals help people?
**Write** about an animal.
**Tell** how the animal helps a person.
**Circle** two nouns you use.

_____

- - - - - - - - - - - - - - - - - - - - -

_____

_____

- - - - - - - - - - - - - - - - - - - - -

_____

- - - - - - - - - - - - - - - - - - - - -

_____

- - - - - - - - - - - - - - - - - - - - -

_____

- - - - - - - - - - - - - - - - - - - - -

_____

- - - - - - - - - - - - - - - - - - - - -

_____

**Home Activity** Your child learned about how to use nouns in writing. Tell about your day in several sentences. Then repeat the sentences slowly and have your child identify the nouns you used.

© Pearson Education

# Nouns

**Mark** the letter of the word that completes each sentence.

1. Mike wants a ____.
   - ○ **A** eat
   - ○ **B** pet
   - ○ **C** where

2. He got a ____.
   - ○ **A** puppy
   - ○ **B** nice
   - ○ **C** when

3. They walk in the ____.
   - ○ **A** here
   - ○ **B** tell
   - ○ **C** park

4. They play ____ in the yard.
   - ○ **A** with
   - ○ **B** feed
   - ○ **C** games

5. The puppy is a ____ for Mike.
   - ○ **A** then
   - ○ **B** friend
   - ○ **C** count

© Pearson Education

**Home Activity** Your child prepared for taking tests on nouns. Read a book together. Point out several simple sentences. Have your child identify the nouns in the sentences.

# Nouns

**Circle** the noun in each sentence.

1. The ice breaks.

2. The dogs walk together.

3. The man gets out.

**Choose** a noun in ( ) for each sentence.
**Write** the sentence.

4. The (where, water) feels cold.

_____

- - - - - - - - - - - - - - - - - - - - - - - - -

_____

5. The (snow, ask) is deep.

_____

- - - - - - - - - - - - - - - - - - - - - - - - -

_____

6. The (sing, fire) feels hot.

_____

- - - - - - - - - - - - - - - - - - - - - - - - -

_____

**Home Activity** Your child reviewed nouns. Have your child write a letter to a relative and circle all the nouns.

© Pearson Education

# Proper Nouns

**Proper nouns** are special names for people, places, animals, and things. They begin with capital letters. **Days of the week, months of the year,** and **holidays** also begin with capital letters. **Titles** for people begin with capital letters. Many titles end with a **period (.).**

**Ronald Morgan** plays baseball. **Mr. Spano** is the coach. The first game is at **Hull School** on **Saturday, April** 28.

**Write** the proper nouns in each sentence on the line.

1. Mrs. Spano gives snacks to the Carver Cougars.

_____

- - - - - - - - - - - - - - - - - - - -

_____

2. Michael plays baseball every Tuesday and Friday.

_____

- - - - - - - - - - - - - - - - - - - -

_____

3. Miss Tyler lives in Tomah, New Mexico.

_____

- - - - - - - - - - - - - - - - - - - -

_____

4. The next game is on Memorial Day.

_____

- - - - - - - - - - - - - - - - - - - -

_____

School-Home CONNECTION

**Home Activity** Your child learned about proper nouns. Go through a piece of mail with your child and have him or her point out all the proper nouns in the addresses.

© Pearson Education

# Proper Nouns

**Write** this note on the lines.
**Correct** the proper nouns.

Dear ming,

    miss tyler watched the game today. Then we went to a restaurant called blue dragon. They have the best food in new mexico. Can you come to our game on tuesday?

        Your friend,
        ronald morgan

**Home Activity** Your child learned about how to use proper nouns in writing. Have your child write his or her name and address. Together check to make sure your child used capital letters when necessary.

**26** Unit 2 Week 2 **Day 3**

**Grammar and Writing Practice Book**

© Pearson Education

# Proper Nouns

**Mark** the letter of the word or words that correctly complete each sentence.

1. Ronald's last name is ____.
   - ○ **A** morgan
   - ○ **B** spano
   - ○ **C** Morgan

2. Ronald goes to school with ____.
   - ○ **A** Rosemary and tom
   - ○ **B** Rosemary and Tom
   - ○ **C** rosemary and Tom

3. Ronald's father is ____.
   - ○ **A** Mr. morgan
   - ○ **B** mr. morgan
   - ○ **C** Mr. Morgan

4. Ronald's nickname is ____.
   - ○ **A** slugger
   - ○ **B** Slugger
   - ○ **C** SLUGGER

5. The team played on ____.
   - ○ **A** tuesday
   - ○ **B** Tuesday
   - ○ **C** TuesDay

**Home Activity** Your child prepared for taking tests on proper nouns. Read a story together. Have your child identify the proper nouns on a page.

# Proper Nouns

**Write** the sentences.
**Capitalize** the proper nouns.

Carver

1. ronald goes to carver elementary school.

_____

- - - - - - - - - - - - - - - - - - - - - - - - - - - - - -

_____

2. He plays baseball every tuesday.

_____

- - - - - - - - - - - - - - - - - - - - - - - - - - - - - -

_____

3. ronald played four games in april.

_____

- - - - - - - - - - - - - - - - - - - - - - - - - - - - - -

_____

4. mr. morgan throws balls to ronald.

_____

- - - - - - - - - - - - - - - - - - - - - - - - - - - - - -

_____

5. The last game is on wednesday, august 26.

_____

- - - - - - - - - - - - - - - - - - - - - - - - - - - - - -

_____

6. That date is near labor day.

_____

- - - - - - - - - - - - - - - - - - - - - - - - - - - - - -

_____

School-Home
CONNECTION

**Home Activity** Your child reviewed proper nouns. Write your child a letter. Do not capitalize the proper nouns. Ask your child to circle the words that should be capitalized and write the words with capital letters.

© Pearson Education

# Singular and Plural Nouns

A **singular noun** names one person, place, animal, or thing.
A noun that names more than one is called a **plural noun**.

duck (one)    snakes (more than one)

You add **-s** to most nouns to show more than one. If a noun ends in
**s, ch, sh,** or **x**, add **-es** to the noun to show more than one.

birds (add **-s**)    dishes (add **-es**)

---

**Add** *-s* or *-es* to each singular noun.
**Write** the plural noun.

1. box  _____

2. owl  _____

3. rock  _____

4. bus  _____

5. branch  _____

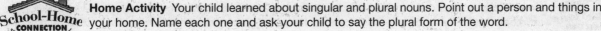

**Home Activity** Your child learned about singular and plural nouns. Point out a person and things in
your home. Name each one and ask your child to say the plural form the word.

Name _____

# Singular and Plural Nouns

**Write** sentences about the story
*Turtle's Race with Beaver.*
**Underline** the singular nouns you use.
**Circle** the plural nouns you use.

_____
- - - - - - - - - - - - - - - - - - - - - - - - -
_____
- - - - - - - - - - - - - - - - - - - - - - - - -
_____
- - - - - - - - - - - - - - - - - - - - - - - - -
_____
- - - - - - - - - - - - - - - - - - - - - - - - -
_____
- - - - - - - - - - - - - - - - - - - - - - - - -
_____
- - - - - - - - - - - - - - - - - - - - - - - - -
_____

**Home Activity** Your child learned about how to use singular and plural nouns in writing. Have your child help you make a grocery list. Ask him or her to tell you which things on the list are singular nouns and which are plural.

**30** Unit 2 Week 3 **Day 3**　　　　　**Grammar and Writing Practice Book**

© Pearson Education

# Singular and Plural Nouns

**Mark** the letter of the word that correctly completes each sentence.

1. A beaver chops down two ____.
   - ○ **A** tree
   - ○ **B** trees
   - ○ **C** treeses

2. Beavers eat leaves from some ____.
   - ○ **A** bushes
   - ○ **B** bush
   - ○ **C** bushs

3. Some ____ can live together.
   - ○ **A** animales
   - ○ **B** animal
   - ○ **C** animals

4. Four ____ live in a den.
   - ○ **A** fox
   - ○ **B** foxes
   - ○ **C** foxs

5. Turtles have ____.
   - ○ **A** shells
   - ○ **B** shelles
   - ○ **C** shell

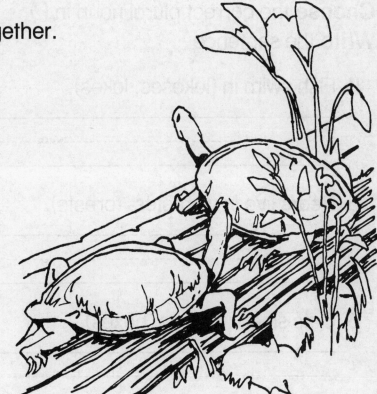

**Home Activity** Your child prepared for taking tests on singular and plural nouns. Read a book together. Have your child find plural nouns that add -s or -es.

# Singular and Plural Nouns

**Underline** the singular noun in each sentence.
**Circle** the plural noun.

1. The rabbits came to the race.

2. The bear cheered for the teams.

3. The turtle saved the trees too.

**Choose** the correct plural noun in ( ).
**Write** the sentence.

4. Fish swim in (lakeses, lakes).

_____
- - - - - - - - - - - - - - - - - - - - - - - - - -
_____

5. Bears live in (forestes, forests).

_____
- - - - - - - - - - - - - - - - - - - - - - - - - -
_____

6. Cats sleep in (boxs, boxes).

_____
- - - - - - - - - - - - - - - - - - - - - - - - - -
_____

**Home Activity** Your child reviewed singular and plural nouns. Together make a list of objects in the room. Have your child write the plural forms of the words on the list.

© Pearson Education

Name _____

# Plural Nouns That Change Spelling

A **plural noun** names more than one person, place, animal, or thing. Some nouns change spelling to name more than one.

| Singular | Plural | Singular | Plural |
|----------|----------|----------|--------|
| child | children | leaf | leaves |
| man | men | wolf | wolves |
| woman | women | mouse | mice |
| tooth | teeth | goose | geese |
| foot | feet | | |

**Choose** the correct plural noun in ( ).
**Write** the noun on the line.

1. A bird has two (foots, feet).

_____

2. The bugs crawl through the (leaves, leafs).

_____

3. All the (children, childs) listen to the music.

_____

4. The (gooses, geese) are noisy.

_____

**Home Activity** Your child learned about plural nouns that change spelling. Together look through several of your child's favorite books. Have your child point out plural nouns that change spelling.

© Pearson Education

# Plural Nouns That Change Spelling

**Write** the plural noun for each singular noun.

1. wolf

_____

- - - - - - - - - - - - - - - - - - - - -

_____

2. man

_____

- - - - - - - - - - - - - - - - - - - - -

_____

3. tooth

_____

- - - - - - - - - - - - - - - - - - - - -

_____

**Write** a sentence that uses each plural noun above. Use words from the box or your own words to describe each noun.

| gray | shiny | tall |
|------|-------|------|

_____

- - - - - - - - - - - - - - - - - - - - - - - - - - - - - - - - -

_____

- - - - - - - - - - - - - - - - - - - - - - - - - - - - - - - - -

_____

- - - - - - - - - - - - - - - - - - - - - - - - - - - - - - - - -

_____

**Home Activity** Your child learned how to use plural nouns that change spelling in writing. Look back at the list of singular and plural nouns. Say a singular noun and have your child say Tand write its plural form.

**Grammar and Writing Practice Book**

© Pearson Education

# Plural Nouns That Change Spelling

**Mark** the letter of the word that correctly completes each sentence.

1. A flock of ____ flew by.
   - ○ **A** goose
   - ○ **B** geeses
   - ○ **C** geese

2. All the ____ ate the cheese.
   - ○ **A** mice
   - ○ **B** mices
   - ○ **C** mouse

3. The three ____ wear hats.
   - ○ **A** men
   - ○ **B** man
   - ○ **C** mens

4. People tapped their ____.
   - ○ **A** foots
   - ○ **B** feet
   - ○ **C** feets

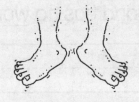

5. Men and ____ danced.
   - ○ **A** women
   - ○ **B** woman
   - ○ **C** womans

6. Does a rooster have ____?
   - ○ **A** tooth
   - ○ **B** tooths
   - ○ **C** teeth

**School-Home CONNECTION**

**Home Activity** Your child prepared for taking tests on plural nouns that change spelling. Have your child look through a newspaper or magazine article and find plural nouns that change spelling. Ask him or her to circle the words.

# Plural Nouns That Change Spelling

**Circle** the plural nouns in each sentence.

1. The horses made noise with their feet.

2. Geese can swim with the ducks.

3. Mice come into the houses in winter.

**Change** the underlined noun to mean more than one.
**Write** the plural noun on the line.

4. The band has no <u>woman</u>.

   _____
   - - - - - - - - - - - - - - - - -
   _____

5. The <u>child</u> followed the boy with the flute.

   _____
   - - - - - - - - - - - - - - - - -
   _____

6. The animals used their <u>tooth</u>.

   _____
   - - - - - - - - - - - - - - - - -
   _____

**School-Home CONNECTION**

**Home Activity** Your child reviewed plural nouns that change spelling. Write the words *child*, *woman*, *leaf*, and *mouse* on paper. Have your child write the plural forms of the words.

© Pearson Education

# Possessive Nouns

A noun that shows who or what owns something is a **possessive noun**. To show ownership, add an **apostrophe** (') and **-s** when the noun is singular. Add just an **apostrophe** (') when the noun is plural.

the goat**'s** legs          the bears**'** paws

_____

**Add** *'s* to each singular noun in ( ).
**Write** the words on the lines.

1. the (turkey) chair

_____
- - - - - - - - - - - - - - - - - - - - - -
_____

2. the (moose) coat

_____
- - - - - - - - - - - - - - - - - - - - - -
_____

**Add** ' to each plural noun in ( ).
**Write** the words on the lines.

3. the (rabbits) tails

_____
- - - - - - - - - - - - - - - - - - - - - -
_____

4. the (animals) plates

_____
- - - - - - - - - - - - - - - - - - - - - -
_____

© Pearson Education

**Home Activity** Your child learned about possessive nouns. Read a story together. Have your child point out possessive nouns and tell what belongs to each person, animal, or thing.

School-Home CONNECTION

# Possessive Nouns

**Write** about members of your family.

**Tell** about each person's favorite color, food, or game.

**Use** possessive nouns to show ownership.

_____

- - - - - - - - - - - - - - - - - - - - - - - - - -

_____

- - - - - - - - - - - - - - - - - - - - - - - - - -

_____

- - - - - - - - - - - - - - - - - - - - - - - - - -

_____

- - - - - - - - - - - - - - - - - - - - - - - - - -

_____

- - - - - - - - - - - - - - - - - - - - - - - - - -

_____

- - - - - - - - - - - - - - - - - - - - - - - - - -

© Pearson Education

**Home Activity** Your child learned how to use possessive nouns in writing. Have your child use sticky notes to label things in your home and show the person whom they belong to. (*Sandra's bedroom, Dad's chair*)

# Possessive Nouns

**Mark** the letter of the word that completes each sentence.

I. The ____ chair was waiting for him.
○ **A** turkey
○ **B** turkeys'
○ **C** turkey's

2. The first Thanksgiving was the ____ idea.
○ **A** Pilgrims's
○ **B** Pilgrim
○ **C** Pilgrims'

3. We ate dinner at the ____ house.
○ **A** Chins
○ **B** Chins'
○ **C** Chin's

4. Both ____ ears began to twitch.
○ **A** rabbits'
○ **B** rabbits
○ **C** rabbit's

5. One ____ breath showed in the cold air.
○ **A** moose
○ **B** mooses
○ **C** moose's

6. A ____ quills are very sharp.
○ **A** porcupine's
○ **B** porcupines'
○ **C** porcupines

**Home Activity** Your child prepared for taking tests on possessive nouns. Write the words *goats*, *bear*, *turkeys*, and *porcupine* on paper. Have your child add either *'s* or *'* and something that could belong to the animals, for example, *goats' food*.

© Pearson Education

Name _____

# Possessive Nouns

**Add** *'s* or *'* to each noun in ( ).
**Write** the words on the line.

1. two (bears) houses

_____

- - - - - - - - - - - - - - - - - - - - - - - - -

_____

2. the (turkey) gobble

_____

- - - - - - - - - - - - - - - - - - - - - - - - -

_____

3. many (donkeys) laughter

_____

- - - - - - - - - - - - - - - - - - - - - - - - -

_____

**Add** *'s* or *'* to the underlined word.
**Write** the sentence on the line.

4. Some <u>roosters</u> feathers are brown.

_____

- - - - - - - - - - - - - - - - - - - - - - - - -

_____

5. A <u>bear</u> fur is thick.

_____

- - - - - - - - - - - - - - - - - - - - - - - - -

_____

6. <u>Rabbits</u> tails are fluffy.

_____

- - - - - - - - - - - - - - - - - - - - - - - - -

_____

**Home Activity** Your child reviewed possessive nouns. Have your child look through a newspaper or magazine article and circle any possessive nouns that he or she finds. Then ask your child to explain how the possessive noun was made.

**Grammar and Writing Practice Book**

© Pearson Education

# Verbs

A word that shows action is a **verb**.

The robot **walks** to the door.

The word **walks** is a verb.
It tells what the robot did.

---

**Write** the verb in each sentence.

1. Pearl enters the science fair.

_____
- - - - - - - - - - - - - - - -

2. Wagner helps Pearl.

_____
- - - - - - - - - - - - - - - -

3. The judge looks at the projects.

_____
- - - - - - - - - - - - - - - -

4. The judge picks a winner.

_____
- - - - - - - - - - - - - - - -

5. The friends go home.

_____
- - - - - - - - - - - - - - - -

**Home Activity** Your child learned about verbs. Read a story with your child. Point to several simple sentences and have your child find the verbs in the sentences.

# Verbs

**Underline** the verb in each sentence.

1. Alex plays with Robin.

2. Robin talks to Alex.

3. They help each other.

**Tell** about a time when you helped a friend or when a friend helped you. **Underline** the verbs in your writing.

_____
- - - - - - - - - - - - - - - - - - - - - - - - - -
_____
- - - - - - - - - - - - - - - - - - - - - - - - - -
_____
- - - - - - - - - - - - - - - - - - - - - - - - - -
_____
- - - - - - - - - - - - - - - - - - - - - - - - - -
_____
- - - - - - - - - - - - - - - - - - - - - - - - - -
_____
- - - - - - - - - - - - - - - - - - - - - - - - - -
_____
- - - - - - - - - - - - - - - - - - - - - - - - - -
_____

© Pearson Education

**Home Activity** Your child learned how to use verbs in writing. Help your child write sentences about things he or she does to get ready for school each morning. Ask him or her to underline the verbs in the sentences.

**Grammar and Writing Practice Book**

# Verbs

**Mark** the letter of the word that completes each sentence.

1. I _____ Ann at school.
   - ○ **A** with
   - ○ **B** see
   - ○ **C** doll

2. Ann _____ the ball.
   - ○ **A** grabs
   - ○ **B** bells
   - ○ **C** school

3. _____ me the ball.
   - ○ **A** Throw
   - ○ **B** That
   - ○ **C** Tom

4. I _____ the ball.
   - ○ **A** cup
   - ○ **B** sit
   - ○ **C** catch

5. Ann _____ for me.
   - ○ **A** then
   - ○ **B** cheers
   - ○ **C** books

6. I _____ the ball.
   - ○ **A** toss
   - ○ **B** and
   - ○ **C** book

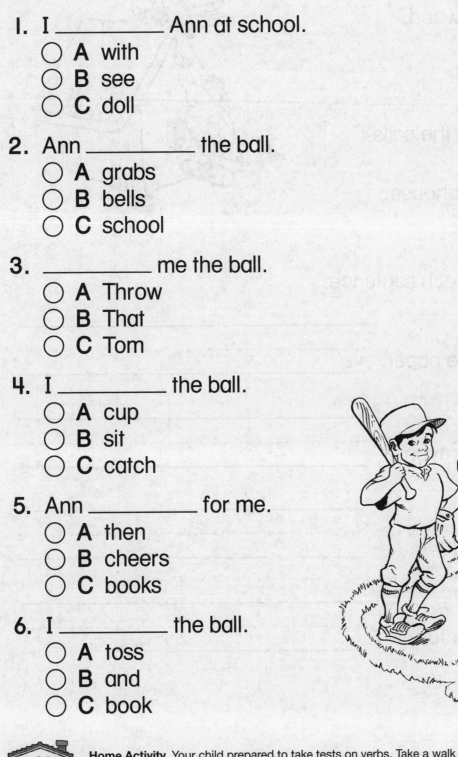

**School-Home CONNECTION**

**Home Activity** Your child prepared to take tests on verbs. Take a walk around the neighborhood and have your child point out verbs that appear on signs and advertisements.

# Verbs

**Underline** the verb in each sentence.

1. John cuts the wood.

2. I paint the parts.

3. Emma pounds the nails.

4. We make a birdhouse.

**Write** the verb in each sentence.

5. Rob finds some paper.

6. Cindy brings crayons.

7. Mia clears the table.

8. They draw a picture.

**Home Activity** Your child reviewed verbs. Write several simple sentences about what you did today. Have your child underline the verbs in the sentences.

© Pearson Education

# Verbs with Singular and Plural Nouns

Add **-s** to a verb to tell what one person, animal, or thing does.

Do **not** add **-s** to a verb that tells what two or more people, animals, or things do.

Juno **writes** a letter.
Max and Pam **write** letters.

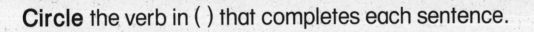

**Circle** the verb in ( ) that completes each sentence.

1. The boy (send, sends) letters to his grandma.

2. His letters (tells, tell) about him.

3. Grandma (like, likes) his pictures.

4. His pictures (makes, make) her happy.

5. Juno (read, reads) a letter from his grandma.

© Pearson Education

**Home Activity** Your child learned about verbs with singular and plural nouns. Look for simple sentences in a magazine or newspaper. Have your child point out verbs that are used with singular nouns and verbs that are used with plural nouns.

# Verbs with Singular and Plural Nouns

**Tell** about things your friend does.

_____

My friend _____

_____

My friend _____

_____

My friend _____

**Tell** about things you and your friend do.

_____

My friend and I _____

_____

My friend and I _____

_____

My friend and I _____

**School-Home CONNECTION**

**Home Activity** Your child learned how to use verbs with singular and plural nouns in writing. Have your child write a note or letter to a relative. Before you mail it, have your child point out the verbs with singular nouns and the verbs with plural nouns.

# Verbs with Singular and Plural Nouns

**Mark** the letter of the verb that completes each sentence.

1. My cousins _____ letters.
   - ○ **A** write
   - ○ **B** sit
   - ○ **C** writes

2. My grandma _____ e-mails.
   - ○ **A** run
   - ○ **B** sends
   - ○ **C** send

3. My sister _____ on the phone.
   - ○ **A** call
   - ○ **B** calls
   - ○ **C** eat

4. My mom _____ the neighbors.
   - ○ **A** sing
   - ○ **B** visit
   - ○ **C** visits

5. My brother and dad _____ .
   - ○ **A** talk
   - ○ **B** talks
   - ○ **C** fix

6. The dogs _____ at us.
   - ○ **A** barks
   - ○ **B** bark
   - ○ **C** boil

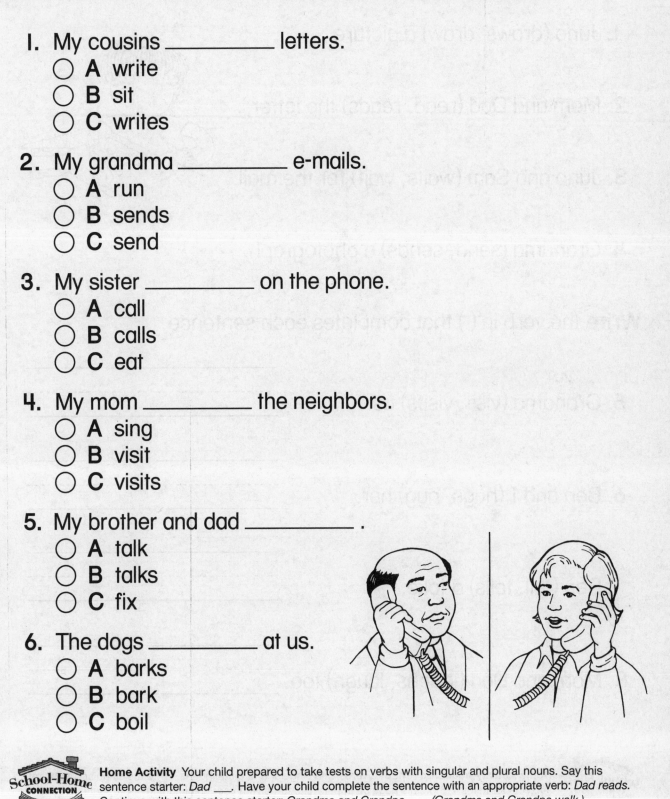

**School-Home CONNECTION**

**Home Activity** Your child prepared to take tests on verbs with singular and plural nouns. Say this sentence starter: *Dad ___.* Have your child complete the sentence with an appropriate verb: *Dad reads.* Continue with this sentence starter: *Grandma and Grandpa ___. (Grandma and Grandpa walk.)*

# Verbs with Singular and Plural Nouns

**Underline** the verb in ( ) that completes each sentence.

1. Juno (draws, draw) a picture.

2. Mom and Dad (read, reads) the letter.

3. Juno and Sam (waits, wait) for the mail.

4. Grandma (send, sends) a photograph.

**Write** the verb in ( ) that completes each sentence.

5. Grandma (visit, visits) us.

_____

_____

6. Ben and I (hugs, hug) her.

_____

_____

7. Ben (tell, tells) a joke.

_____

_____

8. Mom and Dad (laughs, laugh) too.

**School-Home CONNECTION**

**Home Activity** Your child reviewed verbs with singular and plural nouns. Write the singular and plural subjects for items 1–8 on this page on paper. Take turns with your child adding appropriate verbs to the subjects to make sentences.

**Grammar and Writing Practice Book**

# Verbs for Present, Past, and Future

Today Turtle **rests.**

The verb **rests** tells about now. It ends with **-s.**

Yesterday Turtle **rested.**

The verb **rested** tells about the past. It ends with **-ed.**

Tomorrow Turtle **will rest.**

The verb **will rest** tells about the future. It begins with **will.**

---

**Circle** the verb in each sentence. **Write** *N* if the verb tells about now. **Write** *P* if the verb tells about the past. **Write** *F* if the verb tells about the future.

_____

1. Today the spider asks a question.       _____

_____

2. Tomorrow the turtle will answer.       _____

_____

3. Now the turtle takes a nap.       _____

_____

4. Yesterday the spider fished in the river.       _____

_____

5. The turtle walked home.       _____

**Home Activity** Your child learned about verbs for present, past, and future. Read a book together. Have your child point out the verbs in simple sentences. Ask your child to tell you if the verbs tell about the present, the past, or the future.

© Pearson Education

# Verbs for Present, Past, and Future

**Write** about something you could invent.
**Tell** how people will use your invention.
Some verbs you can use are *invent, use,*
*like,* and *name.*

_____

- - - - - - - - - - - - - - - - - - - - - - - - -

_____

- - - - - - - - - - - - - - - - - - - - - - - - -

_____

- - - - - - - - - - - - - - - - - - - - - - - - -

_____

- - - - - - - - - - - - - - - - - - - - - - - - -

_____

- - - - - - - - - - - - - - - - - - - - - - - - -

_____

- - - - - - - - - - - - - - - - - - - - - - - - -

_____

- - - - - - - - - - - - - - - - - - - - - - - - -

_____

- - - - - - - - - - - - - - - - - - - - - - - - -

_____

**School-Home CONNECTION**

**Home Activity** Your child learned how to use verbs for present, past, and future in writing. Have your child write a letter about his or her favorite invention. Ask him or her to underline the verbs and note whether they tell about the present, past, or future.

# Verbs for Present, Past, and Future

**Mark** the letter that tells the time of the verb in each sentence.

1. The turtle tricked the spider.
   - ○ **A** now
   - ○ **B** past
   - ○ **C** future

2. The spider will work tomorrow.
   - ○ **A** now
   - ○ **B** past
   - ○ **C** future

3. The turtle naps in the sun.
   - ○ **A** now
   - ○ **B** past
   - ○ **C** future

4. The spider spins a web.
   - ○ **A** now
   - ○ **B** past
   - ○ **C** future

5. The turtle will eat the fish later.
   - ○ **A** now
   - ○ **B** past
   - ○ **C** future

6. The spider waved goodbye.
   - ○ **A** now
   - ○ **B** past
   - ○ **C** future

**Home Activity** Your child prepared to take tests on verbs for present, past, and future. Write these verbs on paper: *walk, talk, jump, climb.* Have your child use the verbs to write sentences that tell about the present, past, and future.

© Pearson Education

# Verbs for Present, Past, and Future

**Underline** the verb in each sentence. **Write** *N* if the verb in the sentence tells about now. **Write** *P* if the verb tells about the past. **Write** *F* if the verb tells about the future.

1. The spider will fish tomorrow.  _____

2. The turtle will trick the spider.  _____

3. The turtle rested on the bank.  _____

4. Now the spider spins a web.  _____

**Circle** the correct verb in ( ) to complete the sentence.

5. Yesterday the turtle (cooks, cooked) the fish.

6. Tomorrow the spider (will walk, walked) to the river.

7. Now the spider (worked, works) hard.

8. Yesterday the turtle (cheats, cheated) the spider.

**Home Activity** Your child reviewed verbs for present, past, and future. Write *Present, Past,* and *Future* as headings on paper. Have your child write the verbs in items 1–8 on this page under the correct headings.

© Pearson Education

# More About Verbs

Use the correct verb in each sentence to show something happening now, in the past, or in the future.

Today Blanca **fills** a basket. (now)

Yesterday Blanca **filled** a basket. (in the past)

Tomorrow Blanca **will fill** a basket. (in the future)

---

**Choose** the correct verb in ( ). **Write** the verb on the line.

1. Last week Carmen  (plants, planted) a garden.

_____

- - - - - - - - - - - - - - - - - - - - - - - - - - - - - - - - - - - - - -

_____

2. Yesterday the birds (picks, picked) out the seeds.

_____

- - - - - - - - - - - - - - - - - - - - - - - - - - - - - - - - - - - - - -

_____

3. Right now Carmen (visits, visited) a store.

_____

- - - - - - - - - - - - - - - - - - - - - - - - - - - - - - - - - - - - - -

_____

4. Soon Carmen (buys, will buy) a scarecrow.

_____

- - - - - - - - - - - - - - - - - - - - - - - - - - - - - - - - - - - - - -

_____

5. Tomorrow Carmen  (sees, will see) no more birds!

_____

- - - - - - - - - - - - - - - - - - - - - - - - - - - - - - - - - - - - - -

_____

**Home Activity** Your child learned about verbs for present, past, and future. Look through a familiar storybook with your child. Have your child point out some verbs in the sentences and identify whether they tell about now, the past, or the future.

© Pearson Education

# More About Verbs

**Think** of a way that you can help a family
member or friend.
**Write** about your idea.
**Use** the verbs in the box or your own words.

| help | talk | show | need | listen |
|------|------|------|------|--------|

_____

- - - - - - - - - - - - - - - - - - - - - - - - - - - -

_____

- - - - - - - - - - - - - - - - - - - - - - - - - - - -

_____

- - - - - - - - - - - - - - - - - - - - - - - - - - - -

_____

- - - - - - - - - - - - - - - - - - - - - - - - - - - -

_____

- - - - - - - - - - - - - - - - - - - - - - - - - - - -

_____

- - - - - - - - - - - - - - - - - - - - - - - - - - - -

_____

- - - - - - - - - - - - - - - - - - - - - - - - - - - -

_____

- - - - - - - - - - - - - - - - - - - - - - - - - - - -

_____

**Home Activity** Your child learned how to use verbs for present, past, and future in writing. Write these
verbs in a list on paper: *work, clean, dust, sort*. Have your child write each verb three times to make it
tell about now, the past, and the future.

© Pearson Education

# More About Verbs

Mark the letter of the verb that completes each sentence.

1. Rosa _____ tomatoes yesterday.
   - ○ **A** picks
   - ○ **B** picked
   - ○ **C** will pick

2. Blanca _____ a basket now.
   - ○ **A** fills
   - ○ **B** filled
   - ○ **C** will fill

3. Rosa _____ at her garden tomorrow.
   - ○ **A** will look
   - ○ **B** looks
   - ○ **C** looked

4. Blanca _____ to her house now.
   - ○ **A** walked
   - ○ **B** walk
   - ○ **C** walks

5. Rosa _____ on the door last night.
   - ○ **A** knocks
   - ○ **B** knocked
   - ○ **C** will knock

6. Blanca _____ the vegetables now.
   - ○ **A** wanted
   - ○ **B** want
   - ○ **C** wants

**Home Activity** Your child prepared to take tests on verbs for present, past, and future. Have your child tell you about activities he or she does each day, has done in the past, or will do in the future, using verbs for present, past, and future.

Name _____

# More About Verbs

**Circle** the correct verb in ( ).

1. Now Rosa (helps, helped) Blanca.

2. Yesterday Blanca (helps, helped) Rosa.

3. Today Blanca (adds, will added) tomatoes to the pile.

4. Last week Rosa (added, will add) corn to the pile.

**Write** the correct verb in each sentence.

5. Last year Rosa (plants, planted) a garden.

_____

- - - - - - - - - - - - - - - - - - - - - - -

_____

6. Next year Blanca (planted, will plant) a garden.

_____

- - - - - - - - - - - - - - - - - - - - - - -

_____

7. Now Rosa (looks, looked) at her pile of tomatoes.

_____

- - - - - - - - - - - - - - - - - - - - - - -

_____

8. Tomorrow Blanca (looked, will look) at her pile of corn.

_____

- - - - - - - - - - - - - - - - - - - - - - -

_____

**School-Home CONNECTION**

**Home Activity** Your child reviewed verbs for present, past, and future. Have your child write a letter to a relative. Ask your child to point out each verb and identify whether it tells about now, the past, or the future.

# *Am, Is, Are, Was, and Were*

The verbs **am, is, are, was,** and **were** do not show action.

They show what someone or something is or was.

These verbs are forms of the verb *to be.*

The verbs **am, is,** and **are** tell about now.

I **am** a teacher.

Juan **is** a teacher.

Kit and Mack **are** teachers.

The verbs **was** and **were** tell about the past.

I **was** a teacher.

Rachel and Sara **were** teachers.

Use **am, is,** and **was** to tell about one person, place, or thing.

Use **are** and **were** to tell about more than one person, place, or thing.

---

**Choose** the correct verb in ( ).

**Write** the sentence.

1. The plants (was, were) healthy.

_____

-------------------------

_____

2. Dr. Carver (is, are) a hero to me.

_____

-------------------------

_____

**Home Activity** Your child learned about *am, is, are, was,* and *were.* Read a book together. Have your child find the verbs *am, is, are, was,* and *were,* read aloud the sentences in which the verbs appear, and identify the subjects.

# Am, Is, Are, Was, and Were

**Complete** the sentences.
**Use** the verbs *am, is, are, was,* and *were,* along with your own words.

_____

George Washington Carver _____

_____

His inventions _____

_____

An inventor _____

_____

Some great inventions _____

_____

I _____

**Home Activity** Your child learned how to use *am, is, are, was,* and *were* in writing. Have your child use these verbs to write a letter about something he or she did in school. Ask your child to circle the verbs *am, is, are, was,* and *were.*

© Pearson Education

# Am, Is, Are, Was, and Were

**Mark** the letter of the verb that completes each sentence.

1. Carver _____ a great man.
   - ○ **A** were
   - ○ **B** am
   - ○ **C** was

2. Peanuts _____ valuable for many reasons.
   - ○ **A** are
   - ○ **B** is
   - ○ **C** am

3. Inventors _____ hard workers.
   - ○ **A** am
   - ○ **B** are
   - ○ **C** is

4. I _____ an inventor.
   - ○ **A** were
   - ○ **B** am
   - ○ **C** is

5. This invention _____ useful.
   - ○ **A** is
   - ○ **B** am
   - ○ **C** are

6. Cars _____ a good invention.
   - ○ **A** was
   - ○ **B** am
   - ○ **C** were

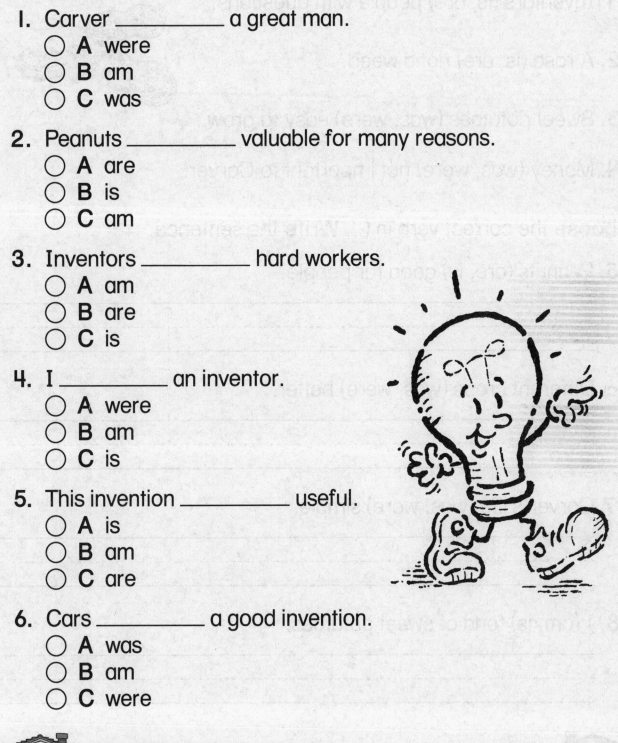

© Pearson Education

**Home Activity** Your child prepared to take tests on *am, is, are, was,* and *were*. Write the verbs *am, is, are, was,* and *were* on paper. With your child, listen to an ad on TV. Try to count how many times each verb is used.

# *Am, Is, Are, Was,* and *Were*

**Circle** the correct verb in ( ).

1. Inventors (is, are) people with questions.

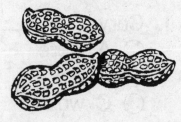

2. A rose (is, are) not a weed.

3. Sweet potatoes (was, were) easy to grow.

4. Money (was, were) not important to Carver.

**Choose** the correct verb in ( ). **Write** the sentence.

5. Peanuts (are, is) good for people.

----------------------------------------

----------------------------------------

6. Different crops (was, were) better.

----------------------------------------

----------------------------------------

7. Carver's life (was, were) simple.

----------------------------------------

----------------------------------------

----------------------------------------

8. I (am, is) fond of sweet potatoes.

----------------------------------------

----------------------------------------

----------------------------------------

**Home Activity** Your child reviewed *am, is, are, was,* and *were.* Read aloud each numbered sentence on this page saying *blank* for the words in parentheses. Let your child tell you whether *am, is, are, was,* or *were* completes each sentence.

© Pearson Education

# Adjectives and Our Senses

An **adjective** describes a person, place, animal, or thing.
An **adjective** can tell how something looks, sounds, tastes, feels, or smells.

> I love **soft** socks.
> **Soft** describes the way the socks feel.

**Find** the adjectives that tell how something looks, sounds, tastes, feels, or smells. **Circle** the adjectives.

1. Mom knit socks for me with yellow yarn.

2. I heard the quiet click of needles.

3. I will have warm feet.

---

**Choose** the adjective from the box that tells how something in the sentence looks, sounds, tastes, feels, or smells. **Write** the adjective.

| crunchy | shiny | loud |
|---------|-------|------|

4. Mom gave me _____ spoons.

5. I ate _____ cereal.

6. I sang _____ tunes.

**Home Activity** Your child learned about adjectives that appeal to the senses. Look around the room. Take turns using adjectives to tell how things look, sound, taste, feel, or smell. For example, *I see _green_ chairs* or *I hear _loud_ music.*

© Pearson Education

School-Home CONNECTION

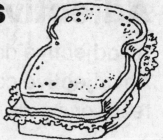

# Adjectives and Our Senses

**Write** the names of two things you can make.
**Use** an adjective to tell how each thing looks,
sounds, tastes, feels, or smells.

| What I Can Make | Adjective |
|---|---|
| | |
| 1. _____ | _____ |
| _____ | _____ |
| 2. _____ | _____ |

**Choose** one thing you can make. **Tell** how you make it. **Write** an
adjective that tells how it looks, sounds, tastes, feels, or smells in
each sentence. **Use** the words in the box for ideas.

| red | loud | sweet | cold | fresh |
|---|---|---|---|---|
| hard | soft | sour | smooth | salty |

_____
- - - - - - - - - - - - - - - - - - - - -
_____
- - - - - - - - - - - - - - - - - - - - -
_____
- - - - - - - - - - - - - - - - - - - - -
_____
- - - - - - - - - - - - - - - - - - - - -
_____

**School-Home CONNECTION**

**Home Activity** Your child learned how to use adjectives that appeal to the senses in writing. Ask your child to circle the adjectives he or she used on this page. Talk about whether the adjective tells how a thing looks, sounds, tastes, feels, or smells.

© Pearson Education

# Adjectives and Our Senses

**Mark** the letter of the adjective that completes each sentence.

1. Dad made _____ spaghetti for us.
   - ○ **A** food
   - ○ **B** spicy
   - ○ **C** turned

2. We gave _____ cheers.
   - ○ **A** loud
   - ○ **B** cry
   - ○ **C** people

3. I could smell _____ meatballs.
   - ○ **A** slowly
   - ○ **B** smoky
   - ○ **C** eat

4. Dad put _____ spaghetti on plates.
   - ○ **A** dish
   - ○ **B** bowls
   - ○ **C** hot

5. _____ sauce covered everything.
   - ○ **A** Thick
   - ○ **B** With
   - ○ **C** Fork

6. We ate _____ spaghetti.
   - ○ **A** cookie
   - ○ **B** gobbled
   - ○ **C** delicious

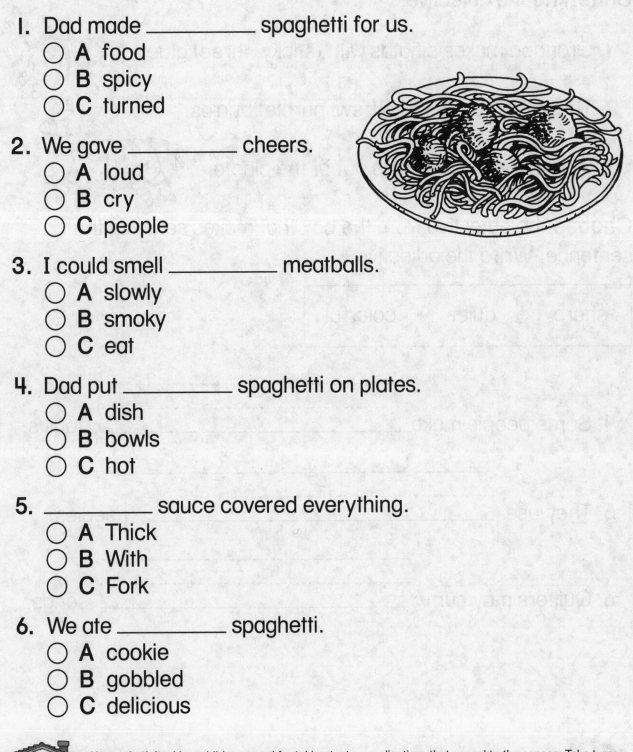

© Pearson Education

**School-Home CONNECTION**

**Home Activity** Your child prepared for taking tests on adjectives that appeal to the senses. Take turns naming a food. Use adjectives to tell how it looks, tastes, feels, or smells or how it sounds when eaten.

# Adjectives and Our Senses

**Choose** an adjective in ( ) that makes sense in the sentence.
**Underline** the adjective.

1. Grandpa makes piñatas with (sticky, three) glue.

2. These piñatas look like (few, purple) burros.

3. (For, Sweet) candy falls out of the piñata.

**Choose** the adjective from the box that makes sense in the sentence. **Write** the adjective.

| sharp | quiet | colorful |
|-------|-------|----------|

4. Some people make _____ quilts.

5. They use _____ needles.

6. Quilters may hum _____ songs.

**School-Home CONNECTION**

**Home Activity** Your child reviewed adjectives that appeal to the senses. Use the words *huge*, *loud*, *sweet*, *smooth*, and *fresh*. Take turns describing things using the words.

# Adjectives for Number, Size, and Shape

Words for number, size, and shape are **adjectives**.
The words **a** and **an** are also adjectives.

> **An** apple has **small, round** seeds.
> The word **an** describes how many apples—one.
> **Small** describes the size of the seeds.
> **Round** describes the shape of the seeds.

---

**Circle** the adjectives that describe the number, size, or shape of something. **Write** the adjectives in the chart.

1. Watermelons have oval seeds.

2. Peaches have large pits.

3. Cherries have one pit.

4. Pea pods hold round peas.

5. An orange has seeds inside.

| Describe Number | Describe Size | Describe Shape |
|---|---|---|
|  |  |  |

**Home Activity** Your child learned about adjectives for number, size, and shape. Look at foods together. Have your child use adjectives to describe each food's number (*two* apples), size (*big* potatoes), or shape (*round* oranges).

# Adjectives for Number, Size, and Shape

**Write** adjectives for number, size, and shape. **Use** the picture to help you decide what kind of adjective to use.

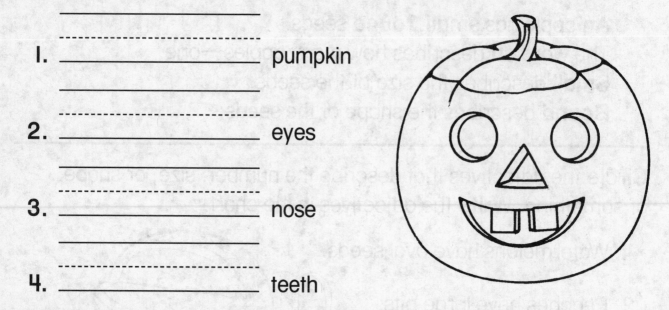

_____
1. _____ pumpkin

2. _____ eyes

3. _____ nose

4. _____ teeth

**Describe** how you would carve a pumpkin. **Use** adjectives for number, size, and shape in your sentences.

_____

_____

_____

_____

_____

_____

**Home Activity** Your child learned how to use adjectives for number, size, and shape in writing. Ask your child to circle the adjectives he or she used in the sentences on this page and to tell if the adjectives describe number, size, or shape.

**66** Unit 4 Week 2 **Day 3**

**Grammar and Writing Practice Book**

© Pearson Education

# Adjectives for Number, Size, and Shape

**Mark** the letter of the adjective for number, size, or shape that is in each sentence.

1. Oval bean seeds were planted.
   - ○ **A** Oval
   - ○ **B** seeds
   - ○ **C** planted

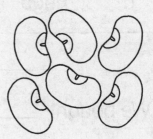

2. Six seeds grew slowly.
   - ○ **A** seeds
   - ○ **B** Six
   - ○ **C** grew

3. Tiny leaves soon pushed up.
   - ○ **A** Tiny
   - ○ **B** leaves
   - ○ **C** up

4. There were five plants left.
   - ○ **A** There
   - ○ **B** were
   - ○ **C** five

5. Then long beans appeared.
   - ○ **A** beans
   - ○ **B** long
   - ○ **C** appeared

6. I saw small seeds inside.
   - ○ **A** I
   - ○ **B** saw
   - ○ **C** small

**Home Activity** Your child prepared for taking tests on adjectives for number, size, and shape. Read a book together. Then go back and have your child look for adjectives that describe number, size, and shape.

© Pearson Education

# Adjectives for Number, Size, and Shape

**Complete** each sentence with an adjective from the box.
**Use** the clue in ( ) to help you.

| a | huge | round |
|---|------|-------|

1. We bought _____ _____ pumpkins. (size)

2. Dad cut them with _____ _____ saw. (number)

3. Mom made _____ _____ pies with the pulp. (shape)

**Underline** an adjective in ( ) to complete each sentence.

4. Pumpkins begin as (use, oval) seeds.

5. Seeds are planted in (small, leaf) hills.

6. The hills have about (dirt, five) seeds in them.

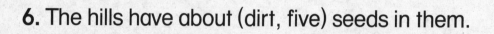

**School-Home CONNECTION**

**Home Activity** Your child reviewed adjectives for number, size, and shape. Take turns with your child replacing the adjective in the first sentence on this page with other adjectives for size. See how many both of you can come up with.

© Pearson Education

# Adjectives That Compare

Add **-er** to an adjective to compare two persons, places, or things.
Add **-est** to an adjective to compare three or more persons,
places, or things.

The bird has **longer** legs than the frog.
**Longer** compares two things—the bird and the frog.

The giraffe has the **longest** legs of the three animals.
**Longest** compares three things—the frog, the bird,
and the giraffe.

---

**Circle** adjectives that compare two things. **Underline** adjectives
that compare three or more things.

1. The young frog is smaller than the adult frog.

2. The tadpole is smallest of all.

3. Young frogs have fewer legs than adult frogs.

**Add** *-er* or *-est* to the word in ( ) to complete each setence. **Write**
the word.

4. Toads have _____ legs than frogs. (short)

5. The legs of a tadpole are _____ of all. (short)

**Home Activity** Your child learned about adjectives that compare. With your child, use the *-er* and *-est*
endings to compare things in the room. For example, say *The chair is bigger than the lamp. The sofa is
biggest of all.*

© Pearson Education

# Adjectives That Compare

**Write** the word in ( ) that completes each sentence.

_____

1. A baby is _____ than I am. (younger, youngest)

_____

2. My legs are _____ than before. (longer, longest)

_____

3. I am the _____ person in my class. (taller, tallest)

**Describe** how you have changed since you were a baby.
**Use** some words in the box to compare. **Add** *-er* or *-est* to the
words when you use them in your sentences.

| strong | old | short | fast | smart |
|--------|-----|-------|------|-------|

_____

_____

_____

_____

_____

© Pearson Education

**School-Home CONNECTION**

**Home Activity** Your child learned how to use adjectives that compare in writing. Ask your child to circle adjectives ending in *-er* or *-est* that he or she used on this page. Talk about what is being compared.

# Adjectives That Compare

**Mark** the letter of the adjective that best completes each sentence.

1. Pond water is _____ in summer than in spring.
   - ○ **A** warm
   - ○ **B** warmer
   - ○ **C** warmest

2. In winter, pond water is _____ of all.
   - ○ **A** cold
   - ○ **B** colder
   - ○ **C** coldest

3. It is _____ under the water than above it.
   - ○ **A** dark
   - ○ **B** darker
   - ○ **C** darkest

4. Algae are the _____ of all the plants in the pond.
   - ○ **A** small
   - ○ **B** smaller
   - ○ **C** smallest

5. The _____ animal of all the animals near the pond is a snail.
   - ○ **A** slow
   - ○ **B** slower
   - ○ **C** slowest

6. Our pond is _____ at night than during the day.
   - ○ **A** quiet
   - ○ **B** quieter
   - ○ **C** quietest

© Pearson Education

**Home Activity** Your child prepared for taking tests on adjectives that compare. Use words on this page that end in *-er* and *-est*. With your child, make up sentences about animals.

# Adjectives That Compare

**Circle** adjectives that compare two things. **Underline** adjectives that compare three or more things.

1. A tadpole is lighter than a frog.

2. A frog egg is lightest of all.

3. That egg is darkest of the three eggs.

**Add** *-er* or *-est* to a word in the box to complete each sentence. **Write** the word.

| deep | high | plump |
|------|------|-------|

4. Frogs make _____ leaps than toads.

5. Toads have a _____ body than frogs.

6. Does a bullfrog have the _____ croak of all frogs?

© Pearson Education

**Home Activity** Your child reviewed adjectives that compare. With your child, choose a favorite animal. Use words such as *taller, longest, faster,* and *smallest* to compare it to other animals.

School-Home CONNECTION

# Adverbs That Tell When and Where

Adverbs tell more about a verb. Some adverbs show **when** or **where**.

A moving van came **today**.
**Today** tells when.

Movers took boxes **outside**.
**Outside** tells where.

Circle the adverb in each sentence that tells when or where.
**Write** the adverbs in the chart.

1. I will never move.

2. I will stay upstairs in my room.

3. Boxes are everywhere.

4. Soon the boxes will be gone.

5. Mom is talking now.

6. We must leave here.

| Adverbs That Tell When | Adverbs That Tell Where |
|---|---|
|  |  |

**Home Activity** Your child learned about adverbs that tell when and where. With your child, add more words to the chart that tell when or where. Start with *tomorrow* and *inside*.

© Pearson Education

# Adverbs That Tell When and Where

**Complete** each sentence.
**Write** an adverb in ( ) that tells when or where.

1. I _____ play with my friends.
   (always, there)

2. _____ we played soccer.
   (Ahead, Yesterday)

3. We play _____ safe.
   (later, someplace)

**Tell** when and where you play with your friends.
**Describe** what you like to do. Use words in the lists for ideas.

**When:** today, sometimes, always
**Where:** outside, upstairs, nearby

_____
_____
_____
_____
_____

© Pearson Education

**School-Home CONNECTION**

**Home Activity** Your child learned how to use adverbs that tell when and where in writing. Together use the words in the *When* list on this page to tell when chores are done. Use the words in the *where* list to tell where something is located.

# Adverbs That Tell When and Where

**Mark** the letter of the word that is an adverb that tells when or where.

1. Today we moved to a new house.
   - ○ **A** Today
   - ○ **B** moved
   - ○ **C** new

2. I like it here.
   - ○ **A** like
   - ○ **B** it
   - ○ **C** here

3. I heard a noise outside.
   - ○ **A** heard
   - ○ **B** outside
   - ○ **C** me

4. Then I saw someone my age.
   - ○ **A** Then
   - ○ **B** someone
   - ○ **C** age

5. We soon went to a park.
   - ○ **A** We
   - ○ **B** soon
   - ○ **C** park

6. We had fun there.
   - ○ **A** We
   - ○ **B** fun
   - ○ **C** there

**Home Activity** Your child prepared for taking tests on adverbs that tell when and where. Read a story together. Have your child look for the adverbs *then* and *now* and for the adverbs *here* and *there*.

© Pearson Education

# Adverbs That Tell When and Where

**Circle** the adverb in ( ) that completes each sentence. **Write** *when* if the adverb tells when. **Write** *where* if the adverb tells where.

1. I looked (around, early). _____

2. (Tomorrow, Downstairs) I heard Mom singing.

   _____

   _____

3. Breakfast would be ready (soon, down).

   _____

   _____

**Write** the adverb from the box that completes each sentence.

| today | here | often |
|-------|------|-------|

4. I _____ have cereal for breakfast.

5. That is what I will have _____ .

6. Things _____ have not changed.

**Home Activity** Your child reviewed adverbs that tell when and where. With your child, make up a story using the words in the box on this page.

# Adverbs That Tell How

An **adverb** can tell more about a verb by telling how an action is done. **Adverbs** that tell how usually end in *-ly*.

> Helen Keller moved **quickly** to lock the door.
> **Quickly** tells how Helen Keller moved.

---

**Write** the adverb from the box that completes each sentence.

| closely | completely | cleverly |
|---------|------------|----------|

1. Helen Keller _____ lost her sight and hearing.

2. Everyone watched her _____ .

3. Helen _____ played pranks.

**Underline** the adverb that tells how in each sentence.

4. No one spoke sharply after a prank.

5. Annie Sullivan slowly taught Helen.

6. Helen eagerly learned finger spelling.

**School-Home CONNECTION**

**Home Activity** Your child learned about adverbs that tell how. With your child, use the words in the box and the words that were underlined on this page. Make up sentences that tell how people do things.

# Adverbs That Tell How

**Tell** about a storm you have been in. **Use** some adverbs from the box in your sentences.

| loudly | brightly | softly | wildly | slowly | fiercely | quickly |

_____
- - - - - - - - - - - - - - - - - - - - - - - - - - - - - -
_____
- - - - - - - - - - - - - - - - - - - - - - - - - - - - - -
_____
- - - - - - - - - - - - - - - - - - - - - - - - - - - - - -
_____
- - - - - - - - - - - - - - - - - - - - - - - - - - - - - -
_____
- - - - - - - - - - - - - - - - - - - - - - - - - - - - - -
_____
- - - - - - - - - - - - - - - - - - - - - - - - - - - - - -

**Home Activity** Your child learned how to use adverbs that tell how in writing. Take turns with your child using the words in the box on this page to tell about storms.

**Grammar and Writing Practice Book**

# Adverbs That Tell How

**Mark** the letter of the sentence that has an adverb that tells how.

1. ○ **A** Loud thunder crashed.
   ○ **B** Thunder suddenly crashed.
   ○ **C** The thunder crashed.

2. ○ **A** I quickly covered my ears.
   ○ **B** I covered my ears.
   ○ **C** My ears were covered.

3. ○ **A** The wind howled.
   ○ **B** The wind blew.
   ○ **C** The wind raged fiercely.

4. ○ **A** I tightly held my teddy bear.
   ○ **B** I held my teddy bear.
   ○ **C** I held my bear.

5. ○ **A** The storm ended.
   ○ **B** The storm slowly ended.
   ○ **C** The big storm ended.

6. ○ **A** I uncovered my ears.
   ○ **B** I uncovered my warm ears.
   ○ **C** I bravely uncovered my ears.

**Home Activity** Your child prepared for taking tests on adverbs that tell how. Take turns with your child making up sentences about family members using the words *neatly, sweetly, nicely,* and *gladly.*

© Pearson Education

# Adverbs That Tell How

**Circle** the adverb in each sentence.

1. I looked closely at the page.

2. I carefully touched the raised dots.

3. Blind people read the dots quickly.

**Choose** the adverb in ( ) that completes each sentence.
**Write** the word.

4. Close your hand _____ .

   (gruffly, tightly)

5. Raise your first finger _____ .

   (plainly, loudly)

6. You _____ made *d* in sign language.

   (correctly, widely)

**Home Activity** Your child reviewed adverbs that tell how. Ask your child to write a sentence using one of the adverbs in parentheses on this page.

**Grammar and Writing Practice Book**

# Pronouns

A **pronoun** is a word that takes the place of a noun or nouns. The words **he, she, it, we, you,** and **they** are pronouns.

**Carlos** is a vet. **He** helps animals.
**He** takes the place of the noun **Carlos.**

**Keesha** and **Paul** are zookeepers. **They** also help animals.
**They** takes the place of the nouns **Keesha** and **Paul.**

---

**Write** the pronoun that can take the place of the underlined word or words. **Use** *he, she, it, we,* or *they.*

1. <u>Len Smith</u> has a sick dog.

_____

2. <u>Len and I</u> will take the pet to the vet.

_____

3. <u>People</u> are waiting for the doctor.

_____

4. <u>Gina Jones</u> helps the vet.

_____

5. "Put the dog on <u>the table</u>," said Gina.

_____

6. <u>Carlos Lopez</u> helped the dog.

_____

**Home Activity** Your child learned about pronouns. Together look for names of story characters in books. Ask your child to replace each name with the pronoun *he, she, it, we,* or *they.*

# Pronouns

**Draw a line** from the underlined words to the pronoun that could take their place.

1. <u>Maria Santos</u> is a doctor.                    We

2. <u>Don and Sara Bell</u> are dentists.          He

3. <u>Ben Waters</u> is a police officer.          They

4. <u>Sue and I</u> are firefighters.              She

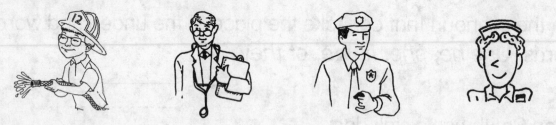

**Write** about someone in the community who helps others. **Use** *he, she, it, we, you,* or *they* in some of your sentences.

_____

- - - - - - - - - - - - - - - - - - - - - - - - - - -

_____

- - - - - - - - - - - - - - - - - - - - - - - - - - -

_____

- - - - - - - - - - - - - - - - - - - - - - - - - - -

_____

- - - - - - - - - - - - - - - - - - - - - - - - - - -

_____

- - - - - - - - - - - - - - - - - - - - - - - - - - -

_____

School-Home
CONNECTION

**Home Activity** Your child learned how to use pronouns in writing. Use one of the numbered sentences above as the beginning of a story. Ask your child to make up more of the story. Help him or her use the pronouns *he, she, it we, you,* and *they.*

© Pearson Education

# Pronouns

**Mark** the letter of the pronoun that can take the place of the underlined word or words.

1. What do <u>Carla and Denny</u> want to be?
   - ○ **A** he
   - ○ **B** she
   - ○ **C** they

2. <u>Carla</u> wants to be a teacher.
   - ○ **A** He
   - ○ **B** She
   - ○ **C** You

3. <u>Denny</u> wants to be a pilot.
   - ○ **A** He
   - ○ **B** She
   - ○ **C** We

4. <u>The job</u> would be fun and exciting.
   - ○ **A** You
   - ○ **B** It
   - ○ **C** They

5. <u>Juan and I</u> want to write books.
   - ○ **A** You
   - ○ **B** She
   - ○ **C** We

6. <u>Paul, Beth, and Ryan</u> are not sure.
   - ○ **A** They
   - ○ **B** You
   - ○ **C** He

**Home Activity** Your child prepared for taking tests on pronouns. Ask your child to write sentences about one or more people and then to replace their names with the pronouns *he, she, it, we, you,* or *they.*

# Pronouns

**Write** the pronoun that can take the place of each group of words.
**Use** *he, she, it, we,* or *they.*

1. Ms. Johnson _____

2. Karen and I _____

3. the fire truck _____

4. Mr. Brown _____

5. the hoses _____

6. Dad and I _____

**Circle** the pronoun in each sentence that could take the place of
the underlined word or words.

7. <u>Dan</u> said he will build buildings.

8. <u>Rudy and I</u> know we will work with animals.

9. <u>Lily</u> hopes she can be mayor.

10. <u>Anita and Rashid</u> say they will be firefighters.

**School-Home CONNECTION**

**Home Activity** Your child reviewed pronouns. Ask your child to point to three pronouns he or she wrote at the top of this page and use them in sentences about community helpers such as firefighters, doctors, or paramedics.

# Pronouns for One and More Than One

**He, she,** and **it** are pronouns that name only one.
**We** and **they** are pronouns that name more than one.

Dale likes to read. **He** has a library card.
**He** is a pronoun that names one person—Dale.

Dale and Jen are friends. **They** will go to the library.
**They** is a pronoun that names more than one—Dale and Jen.

---

**Circle** the pronouns that name only one. **Underline** the pronouns that name more than one. **Write** the pronouns in the chart.

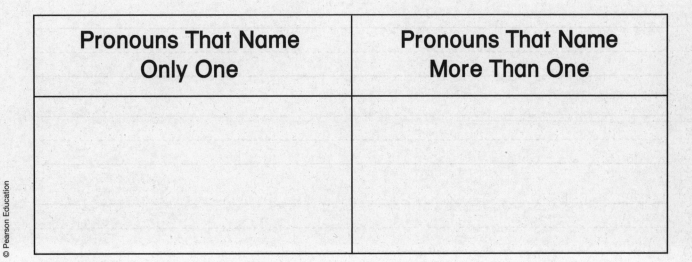

Dale and Jen walked to the library. Suddenly they heard a tiny whine. "We should see what the noise is," Jen said. She went over to a bush. A puppy was caught. Dale pulled it free. He set the puppy down. The puppy ran to a boy nearby.

| Pronouns That Name Only One | Pronouns That Name More Than One |
|---|---|
|  |  |

School-Home
CONNECTION

**Home Activity** Your child learned about pronouns for one and more than one. Ask your child to read aloud the story on this page. Have him or her continue the story by telling what happened next. Remind your child to use *he, she, it, we,* and *they.*

© Pearson Education

# Pronouns for One and More Than One

**Circle** the pronoun in ( ) that can take the place of the underlined word or words.

1. <u>Gina</u> found a lost kitten. (They, She)

2. <u>Leroy</u> helped his neighbor carry groceries. (We, He)

3. <u>The firefighters</u> rescued a family. (They, He)

4. <u>Kelly and I</u> raked leaves for Grandpa. (We, She)

**Tell** about a time you and someone else helped someone or something. **Write** about who or what you helped and what you did. **Use** *he, she, it, we,* or *they* in some of your sentences.

© Pearson Education

_____

_____

_____

_____

_____

_____

_____

_____

**School-Home CONNECTION**

**Home Activity** Your child learned how to use pronouns for one and more than one in writing. Have your child read his or her story on this page. Ask your child to circle the pronouns that he or she used.

Name _____

# Pronouns for One and More Than One

**Mark** the letter of the pronoun that can take the place of the underlined word or words.

1. <u>Greg</u> thinks strange things happen in our house.
   - ○ **A** He
   - ○ **B** They
   - ○ **C** We

2. One dark night, <u>my sister</u> saw a window pop open.
   - ○ **A** they
   - ○ **B** we
   - ○ **C** she

3. One stormy night, <u>Cara and I</u> heard the steps creak.
   - ○ **A** he
   - ○ **B** we
   - ○ **C** she

4. One bright morning Dad said, "<u>Our house</u> is old."
   - ○ **A** It
   - ○ **B** They
   - ○ **C** We

5. One sunny day Mom said, "<u>The sounds</u> are not strange."
   - ○ **A** It
   - ○ **B** She
   - ○ **C** They

6. "<u>The house</u> is just stretching."
   - ○ **A** We
   - ○ **B** It
   - ○ **C** They

**Home Activity** Your child prepared for taking tests on pronouns for one and more than one. Ask your child to make up sentences about what family members like to do and then to change the names to the pronouns *he, she, we,* or *they.*

# Pronouns for One and More Than One

**Circle** the pronoun in ( ) that can take the place of the underlined words.

1. An animal shelter takes in lost or unwanted animals. (It, We)

2. Special people care for the animals there. (She, They)

3. You and I can adopt the animals. (We, They)

---

**Write** the pronoun that can take the place of the underlined words.
**Use** *he, she, it, we,* or *they.*

4. Roy and Rita are new pet owners.

_____

---------------------------
_____ have a new kitten.

5. The kitten must see the vet.

_____

---------------------------
_____ will get a checkup.

6. Dr. Maria Green gives the kitten a shot.

_____

---------------------------
_____ checks the kitten's teeth.

**School-Home CONNECTION** **Home Activity** Your child reviewed pronouns for one and more than one. Ask your child to read the underlined words on this page. Then have your child replace the underlined words with pronouns.

© Pearson Education

# Using *I* and *Me*

The pronouns **I** and **me** take the place of your name. Use **I** in the subject of a sentence. Use **me** after an action verb. Always write **I** with a capital letter.

**I** have a great dog. The dog follows **me**.

When you talk about yourself and another person, name yourself last. The pronouns **I** and **me** take the place of your name.

My friends and **I** play after school.
They see the dog and **me** do tricks.

---

**Write** *I* or *me* to complete each sentence.

1. _____ have a smart dog.

2. Smarty and _____ play catch.

3. Smarty brings _____ the ball.

4. Then Smarty gives _____ his paw.

5. Smarty and _____ shake hands.

**School-Home CONNECTION**

**Home Activity** Your child learned about using *I* and *me*. Take turns telling about animals you have seen do tricks. Use *I* and *me* as you tell your stories.

# Using *I* and *Me*

**Underline** the pronoun in ( ) that completes the sentence.

1. (I, Me) want a rabbit for my birthday.

2. A rabbit will make (I, me) smile.

3. (I, Me) will pet the rabbit's soft fur.

4. Dad got (I, me) a fluffy white rabbit.

**Write** about a pet you would like to have. **Tell** what you and the pet would do. **Use** *I* and *me* in your sentences.

_____

\- - - - - - - - - - - - - - - - - - - - - - - - - - - - - - - - - - - - -

_____

\- - - - - - - - - - - - - - - - - - - - - - - - - - - - - - - - - - - - -

_____

\- - - - - - - - - - - - - - - - - - - - - - - - - - - - - - - - - - - - -

_____

\- - - - - - - - - - - - - - - - - - - - - - - - - - - - - - - - - - - - -

_____

**School-Home CONNECTION**

**Home Activity** Your child learned how to use *I* and *me* in writing. Have your child read his or her story on this page. Ask him or her to circle all the *I*'s and *me*'s. Then tell about a pet you have always wanted.

© Pearson Education

# Using *I* and *Me*

**Mark** the letter of the word or words that complete the sentence.

1. ____ have a fish named Goldie.
   - ○ **A** I
   - ○ **B** Me
   - ○ **C** Mom and me

2. Goldie and ____ watch each other.
   - ○ **A** me
   - ○ **B** I
   - ○ **C** Mom and me

3. One day Goldie surprised ____.
   - ○ **A** I
   - ○ **B** me
   - ○ **C** Mom and I

4. ____ saw her leap out of her bowl.
   - ○ **A** Me and Mom
   - ○ **B** Me
   - ○ **C** I

5. ____ put Goldie back in the bowl.
   - ○ **A** Mom and me
   - ○ **B** Mom and I
   - ○ **C** I and Mom

6. Goldie scared ____.
   - ○ **A** me
   - ○ **B** I
   - ○ **C** I and Mom

**Home Activity** Your child prepared for taking tests on using *I* and *me*. Ask your child to read the sentences on this page and to say the word or words that belong in the blank as he or she reads.

School-Home
**CONNECTION**

© Pearson Education

# Using *I* and *Me*

**Read** the riddle. **Write** *I* or *me* to complete each sentence. **Circle** the picture that shows the answer to the riddle.

1. _____ / _____ am soft and furry.

2. You can hear _____ / _____ purr.

3. What am _____ / _____ ?

**Underline** the word that completes each sentence.
**Write** the word.

4. Mom gave _____ / _____ a kitten. (I, me)

5. My kitten and _____ / _____ play with a feather. (I, me)

6. My kitten makes _____ / _____ laugh. (I, me)

**School-Home CONNECTION**

**Home Activity** Your child reviewed using *I* and *me.* Ask your child to make up another riddle. Use the riddle at the top of this page as a model. Remind your child to include the words *I* and *me* in the riddle.

© Pearson Education

# Different Kinds of Pronouns

The pronouns **I, he, she, we,** and **they** are used as subjects of sentences. The pronouns **me, him, her, us,** and **them** are used after action verbs. The pronouns **you** and **it** can be used anywhere in a sentence.

Morris has cheese. **He** shares **it.**
The pronoun **he** is the subject of the sentence.
The pronoun **it** is used after the action verb *shares.*

Morris met Doris. Morris showed **her** the cheese.
The pronoun **her** is used after the action verb *showed.*

---

**Underline** the pronoun in ( ) that can take the place of the underlined word or words.

1. "Where did you get cheese?" <u>Doris</u> asked. (she, they)

2. "I bought <u>the cheese</u>," Morris said. (them, it)

3. Morris also gave <u>Horace and Boris</u> cheese. (her, them)

4. <u>Horace, Boris, and Doris</u> thanked Morris. (They, Us)

5. "<u>My friends</u> are welcome," said Morris. (He, You)

**Home Activity** Your child learned about different kinds of pronouns. Ask your child to make up new sentences using the pronouns he or she wrote on this page.

# Different Kinds of Pronouns

**Circle** the pronoun in ( ) that can take the place of the underlined word or words.

1. <u>Zack and Max</u> were cats who loved adventure. (They, Them)

2. They climbed <u>the tallest tree</u>. (it, him)

3. Only Buster the dog frightened <u>Zack and Max</u>. (they, them)

4. Maybe <u>Buster</u> could be a friend. (he, him)

**Write** a make-believe story about two animal friends who have an adventure. **Use** pronouns from the box in your story.

| I | he | she | we | they | it |
|---|---|---|---|---|---|
| me | him | her | us | them | you |

_____

- - - - - - - - - - - - - - - - - - - - - - - -

_____

- - - - - - - - - - - - - - - - - - - - - - - -

_____

- - - - - - - - - - - - - - - - - - - - - - - -

_____

- - - - - - - - - - - - - - - - - - - - - - - -

_____

- - - - - - - - - - - - - - - - - - - - - - - -

_____

© Pearson Education

**School-Home CONNECTION**

**Home Activity** Your child learned how to use different kinds of pronouns in writing. Ask your child to read aloud the story he or she wrote on this page and to circle the pronouns in the story.

**Grammar and Writing Practice Book**

# Different Kinds of Pronouns

Mark the letter of the pronoun that can be used in place of the underlined word or words.

1. Ana started a craft club.
   - ○ **A** She
   - ○ **B** Her
   - ○ **C** We

2. Erin and Maria joined the club.
   - ○ **A** they
   - ○ **B** you
   - ○ **C** it

3. Maria wanted Kevin in the club.
   - ○ **A** them
   - ○ **B** him
   - ○ **C** he

4. Kevin liked crafts.
   - ○ **A** She
   - ○ **B** Him
   - ○ **C** He

5. "Kevin can teach Ana, Erin, and me paper folding," said Maria.
   - ○ **A** us
   - ○ **B** we
   - ○ **C** they

6. Kevin joined Ana, Erin, and Maria.
   - ○ **A** we
   - ○ **B** them
   - ○ **C** they

 **Home Activity** Your child prepared for taking tests on different kinds of pronouns. Ask your child to choose three pronouns from this page and to use them in sentences that tell about things that are fun to make or do.

© Pearson Education

# Different Kinds of Pronouns

**Draw** lines to match the underlined words to the pronouns.

1. <u>My friends and I</u> do many fun things.          her

2. <u>Tony</u> climbs high rocks.          We

3. Hallie taught <u>Lisa</u> weaving.          He

**Write** the pronoun from the box that can take the place of the underlined words.

| us | They | it |
|----|------|-----|

4. <u>Josh and Tina</u> build terrific sand castles.          _____

5. Jose drew <u>a poster</u>.          _____

6. Dan helped <u>Angela and me</u> ski.          _____

**Home Activity** Your child reviewed different kinds of pronouns. Find an article in the sports section of a newspaper. Ask your child to circle the pronouns used in the article.

© Pearson Education

# Contractions

A **contraction** is a short way to put two words together.
An **apostrophe** (') takes the place of one or more letters.
Contractions can be formed by putting together a pronoun and
another word, such as *will, are,* or *is.*

    **I will** get some flowers. **I'll** get some flowers.
Many contractions are formed with verbs and the word *not.*
    Otto **did not** read the sign. Otto **didn't** read the sign.

---

**Replace** the underlined words with a contraction from the box.

| | | | | |
|---|---|---|---|---|
| He'll | he's | aren't | shouldn't | I'm |

1. "Signs <u>are not</u> important," Otto said. _____

2. Otto said, "<u>I am</u> going to pick flowers." _____

3. People said he <u>should not</u> pick them. _____

4. Now <u>he is</u> just looking at the flowers. _____

**School-Home CONNECTION** **Home Activity** Your child learned about contractions. Say sentences using the contractions on this
page and ask your child to identify the contraction and the two words that make up the contraction.

# Contractions

**Underline** the contraction in each sentence. **Draw** a line to match a sign and its meaning.

1. Don't park your car here.

2. You shouldn't go faster than this.

3. I'll like eating here.

4. It's time to save money.

NO PARKING

**Write** about classroom rules. **Use** some contractions in the box.

| don't | shouldn't | can't | isn't |
|-------|-----------|-------|-------|
| I'll | we're | it's | I'm |

_____

- - - - - - - - - - - - - - - - - -

_____

- - - - - - - - - - - - - - - - - -

_____

- - - - - - - - - - - - - - - - - -

_____

- - - - - - - - - - - - - - - - - -

_____

- - - - - - - - - - - - - - - - - -

School-Home CONNECTION

**Home Activity** Your child learned how to use contractions in writing. Have your child use contractions to describe some family rules. For example, *Don't leave a mess.*

© Pearson Education

# Contractions

**Mark** the letter of the contraction that means the same as the underlined words.

1.  <u>I am</u> a good helper to my dad.
    ○ **A** I'm
    ○ **B** I'll
    ○ **C** It'll

2.  <u>He will</u> ask me for tools.
    ○ **A** He's
    ○ **B** He'd
    ○ **C** He'll

3.  <u>They are</u> in a toolbox.
    ○ **A** They'd
    ○ **B** They're
    ○ **C** They'll

4.  I <u>could not</u> find a tool.
    ○ **A** can't
    ○ **B** couldn't
    ○ **C** wouldn't

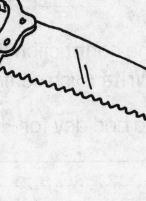

5.  Dad said, "<u>It is</u> next to the hammer."
    ○ **A** It'll
    ○ **B** I'll
    ○ **C** It's

6.  "<u>I have</u> got it," I shouted.
    ○ **A** I've
    ○ **B** I'm
    ○ **C** I'll

School-Home CONNECTION

**Home Activity** Your child prepared for taking tests on contractions. Ask your child to use the contractions *I've* and *I'm* in sentences that tell how he or she helps you.

# Contractions

Replace the underlined words with a contraction from the box.

| wasn't | didn't | wouldn't |
| --- | --- | --- |

1. Hannah <u>did not</u> spill the paint.

_____

2. She <u>would not</u> drip water on Alex.

_____

3. Hannah <u>was not</u> sure about the lost key. _____

**Circle** the contraction that means the same as the underlined words. **Write** each sentence. **Use** the contraction you circled.

4. <u>It is</u> a bad day for Hannah. (It'll, It's)

_____

_____

5. Today <u>she is</u> unhappy. (she's, she'd)

_____

_____

6. <u>We will</u> all help her. (We've, We'll)

_____

_____

**School-Home CONNECTION** **Home Activity** Your child reviewed contractions. Look through a storybook together. Ask your child to point out contractions and to tell what two words make up each contraction.

© Pearson Education

Name _____

# Using Capital Letters

**Days of the week, months of the year,** and **holidays** begin with capital letters.

This year the **Fourth of July** is on **Wednesday**.

**Titles** for people begin with capital letters.

**Mrs.** Davis invited us to a picnic.

---

**Find** the words that need capital letters. **Write** the words correctly on the line.

1. On monday, we went to mr. Jung's grocery store.

_____

- - - - - - - - - - - - - - - - - - - - - - - - - - - - - - -

_____

2. Mom and ms. Jones made potato salad on tuesday.

_____

- - - - - - - - - - - - - - - - - - - - - - - - - - - - - - -

_____

3. dr. Webb marched in the parade on independence day.

_____

- - - - - - - - - - - - - - - - - - - - - - - - - - - - - - -

_____

4. The fourth of july is another name for independence day.

_____

- - - - - - - - - - - - - - - - - - - - - - - - - - - - - - -

_____

5. I wish there were parades in june and august too.

_____

- - - - - - - - - - - - - - - - - - - - - - - - - - - - - - -

_____

© Pearson Education

**Home Activity** Your child learned about using capital letters. Find a calendar. Ask your child to write the names of the days of the week. Remind him or her to use capital letters.

# Using Capital Letters

**Underline** the word that needs a capital letter. **Write** the word you underlined.

1. My favorite holiday is christmas.

2. I like the month of may best.

3. saturday is the best day of the week.

4. Is mrs. Garcia coming?

**Tell** about your favorite holiday.
**Explain** why it is your favorite.

**School-Home CONNECTION**

**Home Activity** Your child learned how to use capital letters in writing. Have your child read his or her paragraph about a favorite holiday on this page. Ask your child to circle capital letters.

**Grammar and Writing Practice Book**

# Using Capital Letters

**Mark** the letter of the word or words that complete each sentence and show the correct use of capital letters.

1. On _____, our teacher had a surprise for us.
   - ○ **A** monday
   - ○ **B** Monday
   - ○ **C** january

2. _____ brought in many small trees.
   - ○ **A** mr. fisk
   - ○ **B** mr. Fisk
   - ○ **C** Mr. Fisk

3. People plant trees on the last Friday in _____ .
   - ○ **A** April
   - ○ **B** april
   - ○ **C** Wednesday

4. He told us it was _____ .
   - ○ **A** arbor Day
   - ○ **B** Arbor Day
   - ○ **C** Arbor day

5. _____ and other parents helped us plant the trees.
   - ○ **A** Mrs. Sloan
   - ○ **B** mrs. sloan
   - ○ **C** mrs. Sloan

6. On _____ , I showed Grandma the trees.
   - ○ **A** september
   - ○ **B** saturday
   - ○ **C** Saturday

© Pearson Education

**Home Activity** Your child prepared for taking tests on using capital letters. Look through a newspaper article together. Ask your child to circle days of the week, months, holidays, or titles of people.

# Using Capital Letters

**Find** the words that need capital letters. **Write** the words correctly. **Circle** the reason why a capital letter is needed.

1. Baseball practice begins on a wednesday in April.

   _____
   - - - - - - - - - - - - - - - - - - - - - - - - - - - - - -
   _____

   | day of the week | holiday |
   | month | title |

2. I was practicing every day in march.

   _____
   - - - - - - - - - - - - - - - - - - - - - - - - - - - - - -
   _____

   | day of the week | holiday |
   | month | title |

3. I even missed the parade on st. patrick's day.

   _____
   - - - - - - - - - - - - - - - - - - - - - - - - - - - - - -
   _____

   | day of the week | holiday |
   | month | title |

**Underline** the words that need capital letters. **Write** the words.

4. Our baseball coach will be mr. Gibson.

   _____
   - - - - - - - - - - - - - - - - - - - -
   _____

5. I will be ready for the first monday game.

   _____
   - - - - - - - - - - - - - - - - - - - -
   _____

6. The game will be on memorial day.

   _____
   - - - - - - - - - - - - - - - - - - - -
   _____

© Pearson Education

# Quotation Marks

**Quotation marks** (" ") show the beginning and ending of the words someone says. The speaker's name and words such as **said** or **asked** are not inside the quotation marks.

"Let's have a parade," said Betsy.
Ross asked, "What kind of parade should we have?"

---

**Add** quotation marks to each sentence.

1. I don't know what kind of parade to have, said Betsy.

2. Abe said, We could have a flag parade.

3. What is a flag parade? asked Francis Scott.

4. We could all wear red, white, and blue, George said.

5. Lincoln asked, Could we all carry flags?

6. Betsy said, That's a great idea.

**Home Activity** Your child learned about quotation marks. Look through a newspaper article with your child. Have him or her circle places where quotation marks are used. Ask your child why quotation marks were needed.

**Grammar and Writing Practice Book**

Unit 6 Week 2 **Day 2** **105**

© Pearson Education

# Quotation Marks

**Add** quotation marks to each sentence.

1. The flag stands for our country, Luis said.

2. LeShawn asked, How do you feel when you see the flag?

3. Erin said, I feel proud.

**Write** a story in which the characters talk about the American flag and what it means to them. **Use** quotation marks to show the words of the speakers.

_____
- - - - - - - - - - - - - - - - - - - - - -
_____
- - - - - - - - - - - - - - - - - - - - - -
_____
- - - - - - - - - - - - - - - - - - - - - -
_____
- - - - - - - - - - - - - - - - - - - - - -
_____
- - - - - - - - - - - - - - - - - - - - - -
_____
- - - - - - - - - - - - - - - - - - - - - -
_____

**School-Home CONNECTION**

**Home Activity** Your child learned how to use quotation marks in writing. Read a favorite story together. Ask your child to point out quotation marks and to tell who is speaking.

# Quotation Marks

**Mark** the correct sentence.

1. ○ **A** "Our flag has many nicknames, said Martha.
   ○ **B** "Our flag has many nicknames," said Martha.
   ○ **C** "Our flag has many nicknames, said Martha."

2. ○ **A** Is the Stars and Stripes one of the names?" asked John.
   ○ **B** "Is the Stars and Stripes one of the names? asked John."
   ○ **C** "Is the Stars and Stripes one of the names?" asked John.

3. ○ **A** "George said, Old Glory is another name for the flag."
   ○ **B** George said, "Old Glory is another name for the flag.
   ○ **C** George said, "Old Glory is another name for the flag."

4. ○ **A** I like the Red, White, and Blue best," Sally said."
   ○ **B** "I like the Red, White, and Blue best," Sally said.
   ○ **C** "I like the Red, White, and Blue best, Sally said."

5. ○ **A** Thomas asked, "Why are there 50 stars?"
   ○ **B** "Thomas asked, Why are there 50 stars?"
   ○ **C** Thomas asked, "Why are there 50 stars?

6. ○ **A** "There is one star for each state in the United States, Sally said."
   ○ **B** "There is one star for each state in the United States," Sally said.
   ○ **C** "There is one star for each state in the United States, Sally said.

**Home Activity** Your child prepared for taking tests on quotation marks. Ask your child to write a sentence about the flag. Tell him or her to use quotation marks and the name of a person mentioned on this page in the sentence.

**Grammar and Writing Practice Book**

Unit 6 Week 2 **Day 4** **107**

# Quotation Marks

**Circle** the quotation marks. **Write** *Yes* if a sentence uses quotation marks correctly. **Write** *No* if quotation marks are not used correctly.

I. "Did Betsy Ross make the first flag?" asked James.

_____

- - - - - - - - - - - - - - - - - -

_____

2. Her grandson said she did, "Hillary said."

_____

- - - - - - - - - - - - - - - - - -

_____

3. Laura said, "I think Betsy Ross did make the first flag."

_____

- - - - - - - - - - - - - - - - - -

_____

**Add** quotation marks to each sentence.

4. How many stars were on the flag Betsy Ross made? asked Barbara.

5. Bill asked, Do you know how many stripes there were?

6. There were thirteen stars and thirteen stripes, George said.

**Home Activity** Your child reviewed quotation marks. Ask your child to rewrite sentence 2 on this page so that the quotation marks are used correctly.

Name _____

# Using Commas

**Mark** the letter of the group of words or the date that uses commas correctly.

1. ○ **A** Littleton, CO 80120
   ○ **B** Littleton CO, 80120
   ○ **C** Littleton C,O 80120

2. ○ **A** November, 12 2007
   ○ **B** November 12 2007,
   ○ **C** November 12, 2007

3. ○ **A** Dear Aunt, Betty
   ○ **B** Dear, Aunt Betty
   ○ **C** Dear Aunt Betty,

4. ○ **A** ski sled, and skate
   ○ **B** ski, sled, and skate
   ○ **C** ski, sled and skate,

5. ○ **A** boots, hat, and mittens
   ○ **B** boots, hat and mittens,
   ○ **C** boots hat, and mittens

6. ○ **A** Your niece Monica,
   ○ **B** Your niece, Monica
   ○ **C** Your, niece Monica

**Home Activity** Your child prepared for taking tests on using commas. Ask your child to name three objects in the room. Have your child write a sentence using the objects. For example, *I see a chair, a picture, and a rug.*

# Using Commas

**Add** commas where they are needed.

1. My seventh birthday party was on August 12 2007.

2. I got games puzzles and some books.

3. We had cake lemonade and ice cream.

4. My sister will have a birthday on Thursday November 29.

**Add** commas where they are needed.

5.     210 Juniper Street
       Pasadena CA 91105

6.              Mrs. Rose Yung
                712 Redwood Lane
                Portland OR 97224

© Pearson Education

**Home Activity** Your child reviewed using commas. Ask your child to write his or her complete address.
Remind your child to use a comma in the address.

# Commas in Compound Sentences

Sometimes sentences have ideas that go together. These sentences can be combined using a comma and a connecting word, such as **and** or **but**. The combined sentence is called a **compound sentence**.

I want to be a cowboy. I want to ride the range.
I want to be a cowboy, **and** I want to ride the range.

I try to rope cattle. I always miss.
I try to rope cattle, **but** I always miss.

---

**Use** the word in ( ) and a comma to combine each pair of sentences. **Write** the new sentence on the lines.

I. I have a cow pony. I need a hat. (but)

_____

- - - - - - - - - - - - - - - - - - - - - - - - - - -

_____

2. I eat beans. I cook them on a fire. (and)

_____

- - - - - - - - - - - - - - - - - - - - - - - - - - -

_____

3. The work is hard. There is time for fun around the campfire. (but)

_____

- - - - - - - - - - - - - - - - - - - - - - - - - - -

_____

- - - - - - - - - - - - - - - - - - - - - - - - - - -

_____

**Home Activity** Your child learned about commas in compound sentences. Ask your child to combine these sentences, using a comma and the word *and*: Cowboys wear boots. They wear hats.

© Pearson Education

# Commas in Compound Sentences

**Add** a comma where it is needed. **Circle** the word that joins the two sentences.

1. Jill wants to be a pilot but she is afraid to fly.

2. Alan wants to be a vet and he loves animals

**Tell** what you would like to be and why.
**Combine** sentences.
**Use** a comma and the word *and* or *but*.

_____

- - - - - - - - - - - - - - - - - - - - - - - - - - - - - - - -

_____

- - - - - - - - - - - - - - - - - - - - - - - - - - - - - - - -

_____

- - - - - - - - - - - - - - - - - - - - - - - - - - - - - - - -

_____

- - - - - - - - - - - - - - - - - - - - - - - - - - - - - - - -

_____

- - - - - - - - - - - - - - - - - - - - - - - - - - - - - - - -

_____

**Home Activity** Your child learned how to use commas in compound sentences in writing. Have your child point out places in a book where compound sentences are used. Ask your child to point to the commas and the word *and* or *but*.

# Commas in Compound Sentences

**Mark** the letter of the compound sentence that shows how to correctly combine the two sentences.

1. Longhorn cattle have long horns. These horns are sharp and dangerous.
   - ○ **A** Longhorn cattle have long horns, these horns are sharp and dangerous.
   - ○ **B** Longhorn cattle have long horns, and these horns are sharp and dangerous.
   - ○ **C** Longhorn cattle have long horns and, these horns are sharp and dangerous.

2. A few big steers are leaders. They walk in front of the herd.
   - ○ **A** A few big steers are leaders and, they walk in front of the herd.
   - ○ **B** A few big steers are leaders but, they walk in front of the herd.
   - ○ **C** A few big steers are leaders, and they walk in front of the herd.

3. Some cows get stuck in mud. They are not left behind.
   - ○ **A** Some cows get stuck in mud, they are not left behind.
   - ○ **B** Some cows get stuck in mud and, they are not left behind.
   - ○ **C** Some cows get stuck in mud, but they are not left behind.

4. Cattle walk slowly. They run fast.
   - ○ **A** Cattle walk slowly, but they run fast.
   - ○ **B** Cattle walk slowly, and, they run fast.
   - ○ **C** Cattle walk slowly and, they run fast.

**Home Activity** Your child prepared for taking tests on commas in compound sentences. Ask your child to choose one of the numbered pairs of sentences on this page and to combine the two sentences to make a compound sentence.

# Commas in Compound Sentences

**Add** a comma where it is needed. **Circle** the word that joins the two sentences.

1. Uncle Kyle has a ranch and he raises horses.

2. Some horses are cow ponies but some are wild mustangs.

3. I chose a cow pony and I rode around the ranch.

4. Later I brushed the cow pony but Uncle Kyle fed her.

**Use** the word in ( ) and a comma to combine each pair of sentences. **Write** the new sentence on the lines.

5. Aunt Liz served beans. I asked for more. (and)

_____

_____

_____

_____

6. The ranch is a great place. I must leave soon. (but)

_____

_____

_____

_____

**School-Home CONNECTION**

**Home Activity** Your child reviewed commas in compound sentences. Read a newspaper article together. Ask your child to find examples of compound sentences—two sentences that have been combined with a comma and the word *and* or *but*.

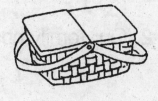

# The Paragraph

A **paragraph** is a group of sentences about the same idea. The sentences are in an order that makes sense. One sentence gives the main idea. The other sentences give details about the main idea. The first sentence of a paragraph is indented.

Every August my relatives get together for a picnic. My aunts, uncles, and cousins come. Grandma and Grandpa come. People come from far and near. We meet at a big park.

**Cross out** the sentence that does not tell about the same idea. **Write** the other sentences in the correct order to make a paragraph. **Indent** the first sentence.

1. First we all open our picnic baskets.
2. Then children play, and grown-ups talk.
3. I don't like grapes.
4. Soon we must leave.
5. Next we eat chicken and fruit.

_____
----------------------------------------
_____
----------------------------------------
_____
----------------------------------------
_____
----------------------------------------
_____

**Home Activity** Your child learned about the paragraph. As you look through a book together, ask your child to point out paragraphs. Have your child explain how he or she knew they were paragraphs.

© Pearson Education

# The Paragraph

**Write** *1*, *2*, or *3* after each sentence to show the correct order.

_____

1. Last we eat tasty treats.            _____

_____

2. Our family has birthday celebrations.     _____

_____

3. We shout, "*¡Feliz cumpleaños!*"         _____

**Write** a paragraph. **Tell** about something special you do with your family, friends, or neighbors. Indent the first sentence.

_____

--------------------------------------------

_____

--------------------------------------------

_____

--------------------------------------------

_____

--------------------------------------------

_____

--------------------------------------------

_____

© Pearson Education

**School-Home CONNECTION**

**Home Activity** Your child learned how to use the paragraph in writing. Have your child read the paragraph he or she wrote on this page. Then ask your child to point to the place where the paragraph is indented.

Name _____

# The Paragraph

**Read** the paragraph. **Mark** the letter of the sentence that answers the question.

Grandma is a terrific baker. She has won many prizes. At the fair last year, her cherry pie won first place. I like to make cakes. Grandma won the grand prize with her cookies. Once a food company had a contest.

1. What was done to the first sentence of the paragraph?
    ○ **A** It was kept long.
    ○ **B** It was indented.
    ○ **C** It had quotation marks added.

2. Which sentence gives the main idea of the paragraph?
    ○ **A** Grandma is a terrific baker.
    ○ **B** She has won many prizes.
    ○ **C** I like to make cakes.

3. What sentence does not belong?
    ○ **A** Grandma is a terrific baker.
    ○ **B** I like to make cakes.
    ○ **C** Once a food company had a contest.

4. Which sentence is out of order?
    ○ **A** She has won many prizes.
    ○ **B** At the fair last year, her cherry pie won first place.
    ○ **C** Once a food company had a contest.

5. What sentence would be a good way to end the paragraph?
    ○ **A** I wonder if Grandma will win again.
    ○ **B** Grandma is tired of baking pies.
    ○ **C** I'm lucky to have a grandma who bakes so well.

School-Home CONNECTION

**Home Activity** Your child prepared for taking tests on the paragraph. Ask your child to write a paragraph about something he or she does well. Have your child read the paragraph to you.

© Pearson Education

# The Paragraph

**Draw** a line through the sentence that does not belong in each group.

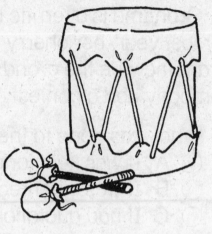

1. I want to be a jingle dancer.
   Jenna wants to be a ballet dancer.
   I will dance at the powwow.
   I will dance to the beat of the drums.

2. Grandma will help me make jingles.
   Grandma will make a video.
   I need four rows of jingles.
   We will sew them on my dress.

**Write** the sentences in the correct order to make a paragraph.
**Indent** the first sentence.

3. Soon I heard the drums beat.

4. Time for the powwow had come.

5. I jingle danced.

_____

- - - - - - - - - - - - - - - - - - -

_____

- - - - - - - - - - - - - - - - - - -

_____

- - - - - - - - - - - - - - - - - - -

_____

**Grammar and Writing Practice Book**

© Pearson Education

# Grammar
# Extra Practice

# Sentences

**Find** the sentence. **Underline** the sentence.

1. In the country.
   Roses grow in the country.

2. The girl climbs trees.
   Climbs trees.

3. The friends play together.
   The friends

4. To the country.
   We go to the country.

5. In a tree house.
   Walter lives in a tree house.

**Write** each sentence on the line.
**Begin** and **end** the sentence correctly.

6. we play games

   _____

   -------------------------------------------

   _____

7. my sister likes tag

   _____

   -------------------------------------------

   _____

8. i won this time

   _____

   -------------------------------------------

   _____

Name _____

# Subjects

**Underline** the subject in each sentence.

1. Astronauts go into space.

2. Six people are on the space shuttle.

3. Earth is a planet.

**Write** a subject to complete each sentence.
**Use** a subject from the box.

| Many stars | Saturn | Space shuttles |
| --- | --- | --- |

4. _____ go very fast.

5. _____ has rings around it.

6. _____ twinkle at night.

© Pearson Education

# Predicates

**Write** the predicate of each sentence.

1. Henry and Mudge hear something.

   _____
   - - - - - - - - - - - - - - - - - - - - -
   _____

2. Henry looks outside.

   _____
   - - - - - - - - - - - - - - - - - - - - -
   _____

3. A big bear walks by.

   _____
   - - - - - - - - - - - - - - - - - - - - -
   _____

4. The bear sees Henry.

   _____
   - - - - - - - - - - - - - - - - - - - - -
   _____

5. Mudge barks.

   _____
   - - - - - - - - - - - - - - - - - - - - -
   _____

6. The bear runs away.

   _____
   - - - - - - - - - - - - - - - - - - - - -
   _____

# Statements and Questions

**Put** a period at the end if the sentence is a statement.
**Put** a question mark at the end if the sentence is a question.

1. Who saw a desert_____

2. I saw a desert_____

3. Did you like the desert_____

4. The desert was too hot for me_____

**Write** each sentence correctly.

5. the desert is dry

_____

- - - - - - - - - - - - - - - - - - - - - - - - - - - - - - - - - - -

_____

6. how do plants get water

_____

- - - - - - - - - - - - - - - - - - - - - - - - - - - - - - - - - - -

_____

7. does a cactus hold water

_____

- - - - - - - - - - - - - - - - - - - - - - - - - - - - - - - - - - -

_____

8. little rain falls in the desert

_____

- - - - - - - - - - - - - - - - - - - - - - - - - - - - - - - - - - -

_____

© Pearson Education

# Commands and Exclamations

Write *C* if the sentence is a command.
Write *E* if it is an exclamation.

1. Come with me.                                    _____

2. I am so excited!                                  _____

3. Wait here.                                        _____

**Write** each sentence correctly.

4. watch the ant

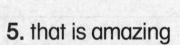

_____

_____

5. that is amazing

_____

_____

6. he is the strongest ant of all

_____

_____

Name _____

# Nouns

**Underline** the noun in each sentence.

1. Two dogs barked.

2. A man fell.

3. The wind blew.

4. The snow was deep.

**Write** the noun in each sentence.

5. The water was cold.

_____
------------------------------

6. The ice cracked.

_____
------------------------------

7. The animals helped.

_____
------------------------------

8. That fire was warm.

_____
------------------------------

© Pearson Education

# Proper Nouns

**Circle** the proper nouns in the sentences.

1. The Carver Cougars play their games at Washington Park.

2. Mrs. Morgan came to the game on Saturday.

3. Did Tom see the game on April 24?

**Write** the sentences.
**Capitalize** the proper nouns.

4. Does ronald like coach spano?

_____

- - - - - - - - - - - - - - - - - - - - - - - - - - - -

_____

5. The last game is in september.

_____

- - - - - - - - - - - - - - - - - - - - - - - - - - - -

_____

6. The team practiced on tuesday.

_____

- - - - - - - - - - - - - - - - - - - - - - - - - - - -

_____

© Pearson Education

# Singular and Plural Nouns

**Underline** the singular nouns in the sentences.
**Circle** the plural nouns.

1. The turtles live in the pond.

2. The rabbits ate all the carrots.

3. The beaver cut down the trees.

4. The animals sat on boxes.

**Choose** the correct plural noun in ( ).
**Write** the sentence.

5. They watch many (raceses, races).

_____

- - - - - - - - - - - - - - - - - - - - - - - - - - - - -

_____

6. The (foxs, foxes) ran fast.

_____

- - - - - - - - - - - - - - - - - - - - - - - - - - - - -

_____

7. Bears climb the (treeses, trees).

_____

- - - - - - - - - - - - - - - - - - - - - - - - - - - - -

_____

8. Birds perch in the (bushes, bushs).

_____

- - - - - - - - - - - - - - - - - - - - - - - - - - - - -

_____

# Plural Nouns That Change Spelling

**Underline** the plural noun in each row.

1. foot      feet      tooth

2. wolves      wolf      leaf

3. child      goose      children

**Choose** the plural word in ( ).
**Write** the word on the line.

4. Many (mouse, mice) build nests in walls.        _____

5. Those (goose, geese) are loud!        _____

6. You chew with all your (teeth, tooth).        _____

7. (Wolves, Wolf) live in packs.        _____

8. Did the robbers have (wife, wives)?        _____

# Possessive Nouns

**Add** 's or ' to each noun in ( ). **Write** the words on the line.

I. my (friend) house

_____

- - - - - - - - - - - - - - - - - - - - - - - - - -

_____

2. her (mother) recipe

_____

- - - - - - - - - - - - - - - - - - - - - - - - - -

_____

3. the (girls) dishes

_____

- - - - - - - - - - - - - - - - - - - - - - - - - -

_____

4. the (ladies) parties

_____

- - - - - - - - - - - - - - - - - - - - - - - - - -

_____

**Add** 's or ' to the underlined word. **Write** the sentence on the line.

5. The <u>cook</u> pie tasted good.

_____

- - - - - - - - - - - - - - - - - - - - - - - - - -

_____

6. The <u>students</u> work was done.

_____

- - - - - - - - - - - - - - - - - - - - - - - - - -

_____

# Verbs

**Underline** the verb in each sentence.

1. The children talk about the fair.

2. The girl works hard at school.

3. The two friends make a robot.

4. Pearl draws eyes on the robot.

**Write** the verb in each sentence.

5. The children wait for the judge.

_____

6. The judge looks at the robot.

_____

7. The robot winks at the judge.

_____

8. The judge laughs.

_____

© Pearson Education

# Verbs with Singular and Plural Nouns

**Circle** the verb in ( ) that completes each sentence.

1. Juno (wonder, wonders) about the planes.

2. Grandma (live, lives) near Seoul.

3. His parents (read, reads) the letter to him.

4. They (smell, smells) the flower.

**Write** the verb in ( ) that completes each sentence.

5. Grandma (like, likes) letters.  _____

6. My pictures (tell, tells) a story.  _____

7. We (mail, mails) the letter.  _____

8. Grandma (smiles, smile) at the letter.  _____

# Verbs for Present, Past, and Future

**Underline** the verb in each sentence. **Write** *N* if the verb in the sentence tells about now. **Write** *P* if the verb tells about the past. **Write** *F* if the verb tells about the future.

1. Anansi will come tomorrow. _____

2. He fished last night. _____

3. Anansi feels full now. _____

4. He will sleep soon. _____

**Circle** the correct verb in ( ) to complete the sentence.

5. Yesterday Anansi (works, worked) hard.

6. Yesterday Turtle (will rest, rested) by the river.

7. Now Anansi (will complain, complains) about Turtle.

8. Tomorrow Warthog (frowned, will frown) at Anansi.

© Pearson Education

Name _____

# More About Verbs

**Circle** the correct verb in ( ).

1. Right now Blanca (needs, will need) flour.

2. Later Rosa (walked, will walk) to the store.

3. Yesterday Rosa (cleans, cleaned) the sidewalk.

4. Now Blanca (helps, helped) Rosa.

**Write** the correct verb in each sentence.

5. Last night Rosa (picks, picked) up the baby.

_____

- - - - - - - - - - - - - - - - - - - - - - - -

_____

6. Today Rosa (rocks, rocked) the baby.

_____

- - - - - - - - - - - - - - - - - - - - - - - -

_____

7. Tomorrow the sisters (hugged, will hug) each other.

_____

- - - - - - - - - - - - - - - - - - - - - - - -

_____

8. Now their mother (smiles, smiled) at them.

_____

- - - - - - - - - - - - - - - - - - - - - - - -

_____

# *Am, Is, Are, Was,* and *Were*

**Underline** the correct verb in ( ).

1. George Washington Carver (were, was) an inventor.

2. Carver's ideas (was, were) good for farmers.

3. Computers (are, is) a modern invention.

4. I (is, am) happy with my computer.

**Choose** the correct verb in ( ).
**Write** the sentence.

5. I (am, is) excited.

_____
- - - - - - - - - - - - - - - - - - - - - - - - - -
_____

6. My idea (are, is) a good one.

_____
- - - - - - - - - - - - - - - - - - - - - - - - - -
_____

7. This toy (was, were) my first invention.

_____
- - - - - - - - - - - - - - - - - - - - - - - - - -
_____

8. Inventions (are, is) important.

_____
- - - - - - - - - - - - - - - - - - - - - - - - - -
_____

© Pearson Education

Name _____

# Adjectives and Our Senses

**Find** an adjective in each sentence that tells how something looks, sounds, tastes, feels, or smells. **Underline** the adjectives.

1. Dad cut bright oranges.

2. I squeezed cool liquid.

3. We drank sweet juice.

**Choose** the adjective in ( ) that makes sense in the sentence.
**Write** the sentence.

4. I build with (sour, smooth) wood.

_____

- - - - - - - - - - - - - - - - - - - - - - - -

_____

5. I hit nails with (loud, green) bangs.

_____

- - - - - - - - - - - - - - - - - - - - - - - -

_____

6. I brush on (happy, white) paint.

_____

- - - - - - - - - - - - - - - - - - - - - - - -

_____

© Pearson Education

# Adjectives for Number, Size, and Shape

**Write** an adjective to complete each sentence. **Use** a word in ( ).

1. I planted _____ seeds. (oval, slowly)

2. _____ vines grew on the wall. (Who, Tall)

3. I counted _____ vines! (pulled, sixty)

**Underline** adjectives that describe the number, size, or shape of something. **Write** the adjectives in the chart.

4. I picked short pods.

5. I snapped open twenty pods.

6. I found round peas inside.

| Describe Number | Describe Size | Describe Shape |
|---|---|---|
|  |  |  |

**Grammar and Writing Practice Book**

© Pearson Education

# Adjectives That Compare

**Underline** the word in ( ) that completes each sentence.

1. The (larger, largest) bird of all is the ostrich.

2. Crows are (smarter, smartest) than robins.

3. Ducks are the (smaller, smallest) of all birds with webbed feet.

**Add** -er or -est to the word in ( ) to complete each sentence.
**Write** the word.

4. The _____ fish of all is the sailfish. (fast)

5. A giraffe is _____ than a lion. (tall)

6. A frog has _____ skin than a toad. (smooth)

# Adverbs That Tell When and Where

**Complete** each sentence. **Write** an adverb in ( ) that tells when or where.

_____
- - - - - - - - - - - - - - - - - - - - - - - - - - - -
I. _____ I leave my house. (Closely, Tomorrow)

- - - - - - - - - - - - - - - - - - - - - - - - - -
2. We will live _____ else. (somewhere, softly)

- - - - - - - - - - - - - - - - - - - - - - - - - -
3. I will _____ have new friends. (forward, soon)

**Circle** adverbs that tell when or where.
**Write** the adverbs in the chart.

4. I packed clothes yesterday.

5. Later I hugged Dad.

6. We drove there on Sunday.

| Adverbs That Tell When | Adverbs That Tell Where |
|---|---|
|  |  |

**Grammar and Writing Practice Book**

Name _____

# Adverbs That Tell How

**Choose** the adverb in ( ) that completes each sentence.
**Write** the sentence.

1. Rain pinged ____. (plainly, loudly)

   _____

   - - - - - - - - - - - - - - - - - - - - - - - - - - - - - - -

   _____

2. I ____ ran inside. (gladly, sweetly)

   _____

   - - - - - - - - - - - - - - - - - - - - - - - - - - - - - - -

   _____

3. I grumbled ____ about rain. (oddly, crossly)

   _____

   - - - - - - - - - - - - - - - - - - - - - - - - - - - - - - -

   _____

**Write** the adverb from the box that completes each sentence.

| brightly | softly | suddenly |
|----------|--------|----------|

         _____

         - - - - - - - - - - - - - - -

4. The gentle wind blew _____ .

       _____

       - - - - - - - - - - - - - - -

5. Then _____ the wind raged.

       _____

       - - - - - - - - - - - - - - -

6. Lightning flashed _____ .

# Pronouns

**Write** the pronoun that can take the place of the underlined word or words. **Use** *he, she, it, we,* or *they*.

1. <u>Our family</u> talked about a fire drill. _____

2. <u>Mom</u> showed us where we should get out. _____

3. <u>Dad</u> said, "Never open a hot door." _____

**Change** the underlined word or words to a pronoun. **Write** the sentence. **Use** the pronoun *he, she, it, we,* or *they*.

4. <u>The Jackson family</u> practiced a fire drill.

_____

_____

5. <u>Leroy</u> ran to the meeting place.

_____

_____

6. <u>The fire drill</u> was a success.

_____

_____

# Pronouns for One and More Than One

**Circle** the pronoun in ( ) that can take the place of the underlined words.

I. One dark night, <u>lightning</u> flashed. (he, it)

2. <u>Mom and I</u> saw a car outside. (We, They)

3. <u>My aunt and cousins</u> ran inside. (We, They)

**Circle** the pronouns that name only one. **Underline** the pronouns that name more than one. **Write** the pronouns in the chart.

Jake and Polly were afraid. They did not like thunder or lightning. Mom pointed to a basket. She reached in. We all watched. Mom took out a puppy. Jake held it. Then he and Polly forgot about the storm.

| Pronouns That Name Only One | Pronouns That Name More Than One |
|---|---|
| | |

# Using *I* and *Me*

**Write** *I* or *me* to complete each sentence.

1. Spot pushed _____ with muddy paws.

2. Now Spot and _____ are both muddy.

3. Dad saw Spot and _____ .

**Circle** the word in ( ) that completes each sentence.
**Write** the sentence.

4. Spot and (I, me) got washed.

_____

_____

5. Spot splashed (I, me) with water.

_____

_____

6. (I, Me) say Spot is a good dog.

_____

_____

# Different Kinds of Pronouns

**Write** the pronoun from the box that can be used in place of the underlined word or words.

| him | They | them |
|-----|------|------|

_____

1. The mice of Mouse School held a Kindness Week. _____

_____

2. The mice children would not tease cats. _____

_____

3. The mice picked Melvin Mouse as leader. _____

**Circle** the pronoun below the sentence that can take the place of the underlined word or words.

4. Melvin spoke kind words to the cats.
   She     He     It

5. "You will not tease cats?" asked Cassie Cat.
   we       they     us

6. "That's nice, but this week is Chase Mice Week!"
   she     it       them

# Contractions

**Draw** a line to match the underlined words with a contraction.

1. "This <u>is not</u> funny," said Lucy.                    it's

2. "<u>You have</u> lost my paintbrush," she said.          isn't

3. "Now <u>it is</u> a big problem."                        You've

**Replace** the underlined words with a contraction from the box.

| I've    didn't    I'll |

4. "I <u>did not</u> lose your paintbrush," said Ken.    _____

_____

5. "<u>I will</u> help you look for it," he said.    _____

_____

6. "<u>I have</u> found it," said Lucy.    _____

_____

# Using Capital Letters

**Find** the words that need capital letters. **Write** the words correctly on the line.

1. july and august are two summer months when baseball is played.

   _____

   - - - - - - - - - - - - - - - - - - - - - - - - - - - - - - - - - - - -

   _____

2. Many games are played on saturday and sunday.

   _____

   - - - - - - - - - - - - - - - - - - - - - - - - - - - - - - - - - - - -

   _____

3. dr. Shea and ms. Wallace took me to a Chicago Cubs game.

   _____

   - - - - - - - - - - - - - - - - - - - - - - - - - - - - - - - - - - - -

   _____

**Underline** the words that need capital letters. **Write** the words you underlined.

4. We went to the game on labor day. _____

5. The game was on a monday. _____

6. We saw mr. Ernie Banks there. _____

Name _____

# Quotation Marks

**Write** each sentence. **Add** quotation marks.

1. Where do we see flags? asked Lewis.

_____

- - - - - - - - - - - - - - - - - - - - - - - - - - - - - - - - - - - - - - -

_____

2. Clark said, There is one on our porch.

_____

- - - - - - - - - - - - - - - - - - - - - - - - - - - - - - - - - - - - - - -

_____

3. I see one in the classroom, Molly said.

_____

- - - - - - - - - - - - - - - - - - - - - - - - - - - - - - - - - - - - - - -

_____

**Add** quotation marks to each sentence.

4. Flags are on the streetlights in town, said Paul.

5. Jackie asked, Is there a flag on the flagpole at school?

6. I saw a flag on a car, Eleanor said.

7. Paul said, I did not see the flag.

8. Are you sure there was a flag? asked Jackie.

**Grammar and Writing Practice Book**

Name _____

# Using Commas

**Write** parts of a letter. **Use** commas where they are needed.

1. Chicago IL 60616

_____

_____

2. March 18 2008

_____

_____

3. Dear Pedro

_____

**Write** each sentence. **Use** commas where they are needed.

4. Tía's birthday was May 12 2008.

_____

_____

5. We had music food and dancing.

_____

_____

6. I got invited Monday April 23.

_____

_____

© Pearson Education

# Commas in Compound Sentences

**Use** the word in ( ) and a comma to combine each pair of sentences. **Write** the new sentence on the lines.

1. Leon has boots. He can't put them on. (but)

_____

_____

_____

2. Use the side tabs. Pull on the boots. (and)

_____

_____

_____

**Add** a comma where it is needed. **Circle** the word that joins the two sentences.

3. Manuel has a white hat and Papa gave him a red bandana.

4. Lisa wears heavy pants but she still needs chaps.

5. Joan bought a jacket and it will keep her very warm.

6. A cowboy doesn't wear pajamas but Rick's mom got him some anyway.

# The Paragraph

**Cross** out the sentence that does not belong. **Put** an X on the line after the sentence that does not belong. **Write** *1, 2,* or *3* after the other sentences to show the correct order.

1. Once he carved a gift for me.

2. Grandpa carves wood.

3. Grandma likes to sew.

4. The gift was a beautiful horse.

**Write** the sentences above in a paragraph. **Use** the correct order. **Indent** the first sentence.

_____

_____

_____

_____

_____

# Standardized Test Preparation

# Language Test

Read the passage and decide which type of mistake appears in each underlined section. Choose the correct answer.

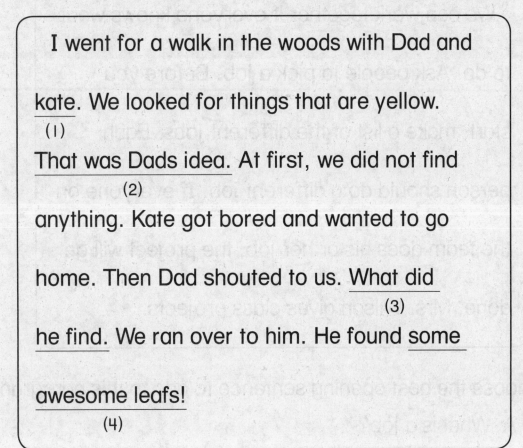

I went for a walk in the woods with Dad and

<u>kate.</u> We looked for things that are yellow.
(1)

<u>That was Dads idea.</u> At first, we did not find
(2)

anything. Kate got bored and wanted to go

home. Then Dad shouted to us. <u>What did</u>
(3)

<u>he find.</u> We ran over to him. He found <u>some</u>

<u>awesome leafs!</u>
(4)

1. ○ **A** Spelling
   ○ **B** Capitalization
   ○ **C** Punctuation

2. ○ **A** Spelling
   ○ **B** Capitalization
   ○ **C** Punctuation

3. ○ **A** Spelling
   ○ **B** Capitalization
   ○ **C** Punctuation

4. ○ **A** Spelling
   ○ **B** Capitalization
   ○ **C** Punctuation

# Writing Test

Read this passage and answer the questions.

> We can work together if everyone knows what to do. Ask people to pick a job. Before you start, make a list of the different jobs. Each person should do a different job. If everyone on the team does his or her job, the project will get done. Mrs. Wilson gives class projects.

1. Choose the best opening sentence to add to this paragraph.

   ○ **A** What is a job?

   ○ **B** Students do class projects.

   ○ **C** Teamwork is important for a class project.

2. Which sentence could be left out of this paragraph?

   ○ **A** Each person should do a different job.

   ○ **B** Mrs. Wilson gives class projects.

   ○ **C** We can work together if everyone knows what to do.

# Language Test

Read the passage and decide which type of mistake appears in each underlined section. Choose the correct answer.

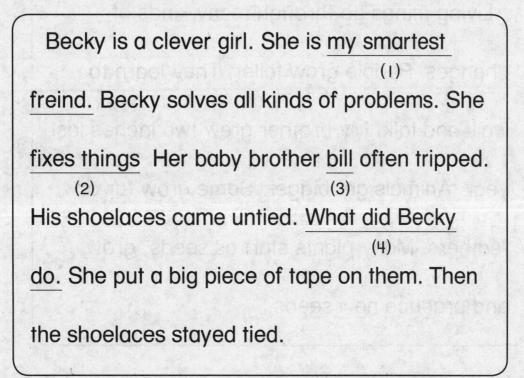

Becky is a clever girl. She is <u>my smartest</u>

(1)

<u>freind</u>. Becky solves all kinds of problems. She

<u>fixes things</u>  Her baby brother <u>bill</u> often tripped.
(2)                                              (3)

His shoelaces came untied. <u>What did Becky</u>

(4)

<u>do.</u> She put a big piece of tape on them. Then

the shoelaces stayed tied.

**1.** ○ **A** Spelling

○ **B** Capitalization

○ **C** Punctuation

**3.** ○ **A** Spelling

○ **B** Capitalization

○ **C** Punctuation

**2.** ○ **A** Spelling

○ **B** Capitalization

○ **C** Punctuation

**4.** ○ **A** Spelling

○ **B** Capitalization

○ **C** Punctuation

# Writing Test

Read this passage and answer the questions.

> Living things go through many kinds of
> changes. People grow taller. They learn to
> walk and talk. My brother grew two inches last
> year. Animals get bigger. Some grow fur or
> feathers. Many plants start as seeds, grow,
> and produce new seeds.

1. Which sentence should be left out of this paragraph?

    ○ **A** Living things go through many kinds of changes.

    ○ **B** My brother grew two inches last year.

    ○ **C** Some grow fur or feathers.

2. Choose the best sentence to end this paragraph.

    ○ **A** Plants are more interesting than animals.

    ○ **B** People learn many things.

    ○ **C** All living things grow and change.

# Language Test

Read the passage and decide which type of mistake appears in each underlined section. Choose the correct answer.

> In june, Maria had a great idea. She
> _____
> (1)
> asked her friends, Would you like to build a
> _____
> (2)
> clubhouse?" Paula answered, "I want only girls
> in the club." The others decided the clubhouse
> should be for eveyone. Then Maria, Donnie
> _____        _____
>                (3)
> Ruth, and Phil built a clubhouse. They invited
> _____
>       (4)
> Paula to join them.

I. ○ **A** Spelling

○ **B** Capitalization

○ **C** Punctuation

2. ○ **A** Spelling

○ **B** Capitalization

○ **C** Punctuation

3. ○ **A** Spelling

○ **B** Capitalization

○ **C** Punctuation

4. ○ **A** Spelling

○ **B** Capitalization

○ **C** Punctuation

# Writing Test

Read this passage and answer the questions.

> (1) On New Year's Day, each person in our family writes a good wish for the other people in the family. (2) The papers go in a special box. (3) The next New Year's Eve, we open the box and read the good wishes. (4) Sometimes the wishes come true. (5) We all feel loved and special.

**1.** Choose the best opening sentence to add to this paragraph.

○ **A** New Year's Day is a holiday.

○ **B** What celebrations are important to you?

○ **C** Our family has a special tradition.

**2.** Where is the best place to add this sentence?

**We keep what we write a secret.**

○ **A** Before sentence 1

○ **B** Between sentences 1 and 2

○ **C** After sentence 4

**Grammar and Writing Practice Book**

© Pearson Education

# Unit Writing Lessons

Name _____

# Story Chart

Fill out this story chart to help you organize your ideas.

Title _____

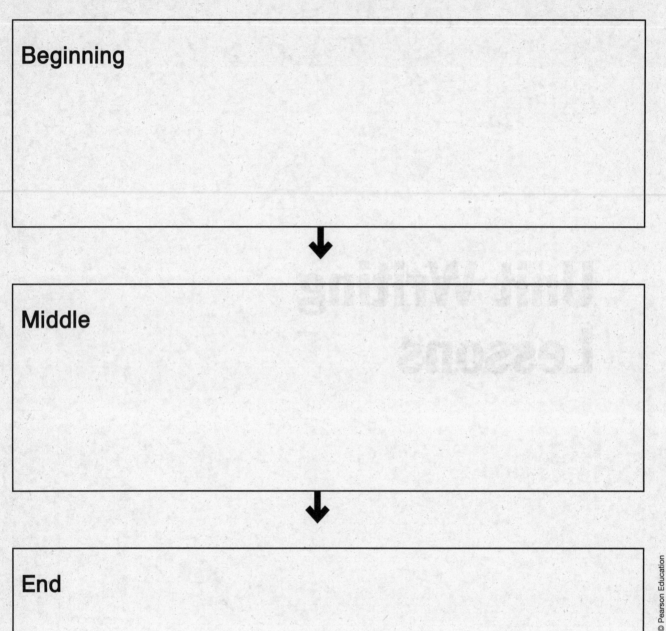

**Beginning**

**Middle**

**End**

© Pearson Education

Name _____

# Use Words That Tell How You Feel

**Write** a word from the box to tell how the writer feels.
**Use** each word one time.

| Word Bank |
| --- |
| nervous |
| mad |
| scared |
| excited |

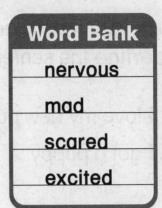

_____

1. I am _____.
   I am getting a new puppy.

_____

2. José is _____.
   Tim took his favorite toy car.

_____

3. The boys are _____.
   They heard a strange sound.

_____

4. Jackie feels _____.
   She is trying out for the play.

© Pearson Education

Name _____

# Writing Trait: Voice

Which sentence in each pair tells more about how the writer feels?
**Underline** the sentence.

1. I love my new puppy.

   I got a puppy.

2. I exercise every day.

   Exercise makes me feel good.

3. The party was nice.

   That was the most amazing party ever!

4. Tears poured down my face after the movie.

   The movie was sad.

5. My hands shook and my stomach flopped over.

   I was scared.

© Pearson Education

**Grammar and Writing Practice Book**

Name _____

# Self-Evaluation Guide

**Check** *Yes* or *No* about voice in your story.

|  | Yes | No |
|---|---|---|
| I. I used words that tell how I feel. | | |
| 2. I used one or more words that describe. | | |
| 3. I used one or more words that show action. | | |

**Answer** the questions.

4. What is the best part of your story?

_____

_____

_____

_____

5. What is one thing you would change about this story if you could write it again?

_____

_____

_____

_____

Name _____

# How-to Chart

Fill out this how-to chart to help you organize your ideas.

Title _____

Step 1

↓

Step 2

↓

Step 3

↓

Step 4

Name _____

# Use Strong Verbs

**Write** a verb from the word bank that gives a clear picture of what to do.

**Word Bank**
Chill
Peel
Scratch
Glue
Decorate

1. _____ your frame with beans, buttons, and glitter.

2. _____ the lemonade in the refrigerator.

3. _____ the paint off with a toothpick.

4. _____ the skin off the apple.

5. _____ the ends of the paper strips together.

© Pearson Education

Name _____

# Writing Trait: Organization

Put the steps in the order they happened.
**Write** a time-order word from the word
bank to complete each step.

| Word Bank |
|---|
| First |
| Next |
| Then |
| Last |

## How to Make a Frozen Yogurt Sundae

_____
-----------------------------
_____, add your favorite fruit toppings.


_____
-----------------------------
_____, take frozen yogurt out of the freezer.


_____
-----------------------------
_____, eat your delicious yogurt sundae.


_____
-----------------------------
_____, scoop frozen yogurt into a dish.

© Pearson Education

Name _____

# Self-Evaluation Guide

**Check** *Yes* or *No* about organization and word choice in your report.

|  | Yes | No |
|---|---|---|
| 1. I wrote the steps in the correct order. |  |  |
| 2. I used one or more time-order words to show the order. |  |  |
| 3. I used one or more strong verbs to tell what to do. |  |  |

**Answer** the questions.

4. What is the best part of your report?

_____

---------------------------------------

_____

---------------------------------------

_____

---------------------------------------

_____

5. What is one thing you would change about this report if you could write it again?

_____

---------------------------------------

_____

---------------------------------------

_____

---------------------------------------

_____

Name _____

# Compare and Contrast T-Chart

**Fill out** this chart to help you organize your ideas.

_____

- - - - - - - - - - - - - - - - - - - - - - - - - - - - - - - -

**Introduction** _____

_____

- - - - - - - - - - - - - - - - - - - - - - - - - - - - - - - -

_____

| Alike | Different |
|---|---|
|  |  |
|  |  |
|  |  |
|  |  |
|  |  |

_____

- - - - - - - - - - - - - - - - - - - - - - - - - - - - - - - -

**Conclusion** _____

_____

- - - - - - - - - - - - - - - - - - - - - - - - - - - - - - - -

_____

Name _____

# Use Words That Compare and Contrast

**Read** each set of sentences.
**Write** a word from the box to complete the last sentence.
**Use** each word one time.

**Word Bank**

and

like

too

but

unlike

**1.** I like art class. My sister does not.

_____

- - - - - - - - - - - - - - - - - - - - - - -

I like art class, _____ my sister does not.

**2.** My sister's ballet lesson is at noon. My lesson is at 1:00.

_____

- - - - - - - - - - - - - - - - - - - - - - -

My sister's ballet lesson is at noon, _____ my lesson is at 1:00.

**3.** I drew purple flowers. Maria drew purple flowers.

_____

- - - - - - - - - - - - - - - - - - - - - - -

_____ Maria, I drew purple flowers.

**4.** Nate made a clay pot. I made a clay plate.

_____

- - - - - - - - - - - - - - - - - - - - - - -

_____ Nathan, I made a clay plate.

**5.** Pearl has a robot. Wagner has a robot.

_____

- - - - - - - - - - - - - - - - - - - - - - -

Pearl has a robot, and Wagner has a robot _____.

Name _____

# Writing Trait: Sentences

- Use all kinds of sentences: statements, questions, commands, and exclamations.
- Use different beginnings. Don't start too many sentences with *the, he,* or *she.*

**Write** the letter of each sentence next to the word that says what kind of sentence it is.

(A) Who made that painting? (B) I think it is beautiful!
(C) Look at the bright colors. (D) The artist shows what a sunset looks like.

1. Statement: _____          3. Command: _____

2. Question: _____          4. Exclamation: _____

**Rearrange** the words in each sentence so that it begins with a different word. **Write** the new sentences.

    **Example**: He has collected rocks for several years.
            For several years he has collected rocks.

    He brought his rock collection to school today. He showed us the rocks after lunch. He will show them to another class tomorrow.

_____

_____

_____

_____

_____

© Pearson Education

Name _____

# Self-Evaluation Guide

**Check** *Yes* or *No* about sentences in your essay.

|  | Yes | No |
|---|---|---|
| 1. I used different kinds of sentences. | | |
| 2. I used different beginnings for my sentences. | | |
| 3. I used short sentences and long sentences. | | |

**Answer** the questions.

4. What is the best part of your essay?

_____

_____

_____

_____

_____

5. What is one thing you would change about this essay if you could write it again?

_____

_____

_____

_____

© Pearson Education

Name _____

# Details Web

Fill out this details web to help you organize your ideas.

Name _____

# Use Strong Adjectives

**Look** at the adjectives in dark type.
**Which** sentence in each pair has a stronger adjective?
**Underline** the sentence.

1. We looked at the **colorful** garden.

   We looked at the **pretty** garden.

2. She ate a **good** apple.

   She ate a **crisp** apple.

3. My grandmother made me a **nice** quilt.

   My grandmother made me a **blue and white** quilt.

4. The thunder made a **booming** sound.

   The thunder made a **loud** sound.

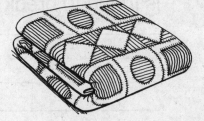

5. The pumpkin pie smelled **good**.

   The pumpkin pie smelled **spicy**.

© Pearson Education

Name _____

# Writing Trait: Focus/Ideas

Which sentence in each paragraph does NOT belong?
**Draw** a line through that sentence.
**Add** a sentence that does belong in the paragraph.
**Write** your sentence on the line.

1. The new park in our neighborhood is a great place to play. It has a baseball field. The climbing set has long tunnels. A dog was in the park. The basketball court doesn't have any cracks in it!

   _____
   - - - - - - - - - - - - - - - - - - - - - - - - - - - - - - - - -
   _____
   - - - - - - - - - - - - - - - - - - - - - - - - - - - - - - - - -
   _____

2. The hen lays an egg. Then she sits on the egg to keep it warm. The rooster crows loudly. The egg starts to hatch. A baby chick is trying to break out of the egg.

   _____
   - - - - - - - - - - - - - - - - - - - - - - - - - - - - - - - - -
   _____
   - - - - - - - - - - - - - - - - - - - - - - - - - - - - - - - - -
   _____

3. We are moving to a new town because Dad got a new job. I wish I didn't have to leave my friends. Dad says I will make new friends. Mr. Hanson is our next-door neighbor.

   _____
   - - - - - - - - - - - - - - - - - - - - - - - - - - - - - - - - -
   _____

Name _____

# Self-Evaluation Guide

**Check** *Yes* or *No* about focus/ideas in your description.

|  | Yes | No |
|---|---|---|
| 1. All my sentences tell about my topic. |  |  |
| 2. I used one or more strong adjectives. |  |  |
| 3. I used one or more action verbs. |  |  |

**Answer** the questions.

4. What is the best part of your description?

_____
_____
_____
_____
_____
_____

5. What is one thing you would change about this description if you could write it again?

_____
_____
_____
_____
_____
_____

© Pearson Education

Name _____

# Persuasion Chart

Fill out this persuasion chart to help you organize your ideas.

Topic    I want _____ to _____.
         (audience)                        (purpose)

**Brainstorm** reasons here.

_____
- - - - - - - - - - - - - - - - - - - -
_____
- - - - - - - - - - - - - - - - - - - -
_____
- - - - - - - - - - - - - - - - - - - -
_____
- - - - - - - - - - - - - - - - - - - -
_____
- - - - - - - - - - - - - - - - - - - -
_____

**Organize** your reasons here.

Least important                    Most important

_____          _____
- - - - - - - - - - - - - - - -    - - - - - - - - - - - - - - - -
_____          _____
- - - - - - - - - - - - - - - -    - - - - - - - - - - - - - - - -
_____          _____
- - - - - - - - - - - - - - - -    - - - - - - - - - - - - - - - -
_____          _____
- - - - - - - - - - - - - - - -    - - - - - - - - - - - - - - - -
_____          _____

© Pearson Education

Name _____

# Use Persuasive Words

Use words from the box to complete
the letter.

**Word Bank**

- important
- best
- need
- should

April 4, 2007

Dear Dad,

_____

I think we _____ make a trip to Water World.

We can slide down the Zoom Tube and swim in the Swirl Pool. That

_____

would be the _____ thing to do on a hot summer day.

_____

We have all been working hard, and we _____ a treat.

_____

Also, it is _____ for us to spend time together.

Your son,

Andrew

Name _____

# Writing Trait: Word Choice

**Underline** the sentence in each pair that sounds more interesting.

Snow was in the yard.

**Snow** blanketed the yard.

The boy whispered his name.

**The** boy said his name.

Those flowers are pretty.

**Those** roses are bright red.

**Rewrite** the following sentences to make them more interesting.
You can change and add words.

1. The dog was nice.

_____

- - - - - - - - - - - - - - - - - - - - - - - - - - - - - - - -

_____

- - - - - - - - - - - - - - - - - - - - - - - - - - - - - - - -

_____

2. I rode on my bike.

_____

- - - - - - - - - - - - - - - - - - - - - - - - - - - - - - - -

_____

- - - - - - - - - - - - - - - - - - - - - - - - - - - - - - - -

_____

Name _____

# Self-Evaluation Guide

**Check** *Yes* or *No* about word choice in your letter.

|  | Yes | No |
|---|---|---|
| I. I used one or more words to persuade. |  |  |
| 2. I used one or more good adjectives to describe. |  |  |
| 3. I used exact words instead of vague ones such as *nice*. |  |  |

**Answer** the questions.

4. What is the best part of your letter?

_____

_____

_____

_____

5. What is one thing you would change about this letter if you could write it again?

_____

_____

_____

_____

Name _____

# K-W-L Chart

Fill out this K-W-L chart to help you organize your ideas.

| What I Know | What I Want to Know | What I Learned |
|---|---|---|
| | | |
| | | |
| | | |

Name _____

# Eliminate Wordiness

Don't use more words than are needed.

• Take out phrases such as *kind of, I think that,* and *it seems like*.

• Don't use *a lot of*. Use *many* or another word.

• Don't use two words that mean the same thing: ~~great~~ big, ~~little~~ tiny.

• Don't use several words when you can use one word: moved ~~with great slowness~~, move slowly.

**Look** at each pair of sentences. **Write** the words that are left out in the second sentence.

1. Aaron is wearing a great big cowboy hat.
   Aaron is wearing a big cowboy hat.

   _____

   - - - - - - - - - - - - - - - - - - - - - - - - - - - - - - -

   _____

2. I think that Beth is kind of excited.
   Beth is excited.

   _____

   - - - - - - - - - - - - - - - - - - - - - - - - - - - - - - -

   _____

**Look** at each pair of sentences. **Circle** the word that is different in the second sentence. **Write** the words that the word replaced.

3. The children played a lot of baseball games.
   The children played ten baseball games.

   _____

   - - - - - - - - - - - - - - - - - - - - - - - - - - - - - - -

   _____

4. She carried the flag with a great deal of care.
   She carried the flag carefully.

   _____

   - - - - - - - - - - - - - - - - - - - - - - - - - - - - - - -

   _____

© Pearson Education

Name _____

# Writing Trait: Paragraph

- All the sentences in a paragraph must tell about the same idea.
- The sentences in a paragraph must be in an order that makes sense.
- One sentence in a paragraph gives the main idea, and the other sentences give details about the main idea.
- The first sentence of a paragraph is indented.

**Read** the sentences below. **Cross out** the sentence that does not tell about the same idea. **Write** the other sentences in the correct order to make a paragraph. **Indent** the first sentence.

Chris swung her bat at the ball.
She waited for the first pitch.
Chris raced to first base.
Her team won five games.
Whack! The bat hit the ball.
It was Chris's turn to bat.

_____

- - - - - - - - - - - - - - - - - - - - - - - - - - - - - - - - - - -

_____

- - - - - - - - - - - - - - - - - - - - - - - - - - - - - - - - - - -

_____

- - - - - - - - - - - - - - - - - - - - - - - - - - - - - - - - - - -

_____

- - - - - - - - - - - - - - - - - - - - - - - - - - - - - - - - - - -

_____

- - - - - - - - - - - - - - - - - - - - - - - - - - - - - - - - - - -

_____

- - - - - - - - - - - - - - - - - - - - - - - - - - - - - - - - - - -

Name _____

# Self-Evaluation Guide

**Check** *Yes* or *No* about paragraphs in your research report.

|  | Yes | No |
|---|---|---|
| 1. I organized my facts in paragraphs. |  |  |
| 2. The sentences in my paragraphs are in an order that makes sense. |  |  |
| 3. The sentences in each paragraph tell about the same idea. |  |  |

**Answer** the questions.

4. What is the best part of your research report?

_____

_____

_____

_____

_____

_____

5. What is one thing you would change about this research report if you could write it again?

_____

_____

_____

_____

_____

_____

© Pearson Education